Requiem of Lost Souls

Kristina Howells

Allies Press
Copyright 2017 Kristina Howells
All rights reserved
Printed in the European Union
All artwork in this book other than sources mentioned are done by Kristina
Howells
ISBN 978-0-244-30763-9
For additional copies please order online at: www.lulu.com

*****

Requiem of Lost Souls

*****

Requiem: Kristina Howells

This Requiem has been composed and written in order to remember the end of WW1. It was thought that this war would end all wars, and as we see it hasn't. The wars continue. This Requiem has been written to represent the pain and suffering of modern times, and how it still exists.

About the Composer

Kristina Howells originally from Dunstable, Great Britain, has dedicated her life to music, and writing. She began her musical studies at the Junior Guildhall School of Music and Drama where she studied, voice and piano, as well as composition, before obtaining her degree at Brunel University London, and Post Graduate Certificate of Music Education at Middlesex University London.

Following her studies she has written a large collection of books, both fiction and nonfiction. She has had two poetry collections published and several songs that she has written, including instrumental pieces. Her orchestral work Calm was accepted by the Royal Philharmonic Orchestra new composer's workshop in 2001 Nottingham that was performed as part of the East Midlands COMA workshops to which she was a member of.

Requiem of Lost Souls is her first ever choral work that she has both written and composed, aided by Frédéric Bara. Her childhood dream of composing her first choral work has finally become a reality.

Her musical works include:

Calm
Secret and Lies
Pride and Prejudice Suite
Collection of Songs
Suite for Piano and Viola
Calm
Violin Concerto
Symphony
Ann Boleyn Operetta

Index

Rest Eternal
Requiem of Lost Souls

Lyrics by: Kristina Howells

Music by: Kristina Howells

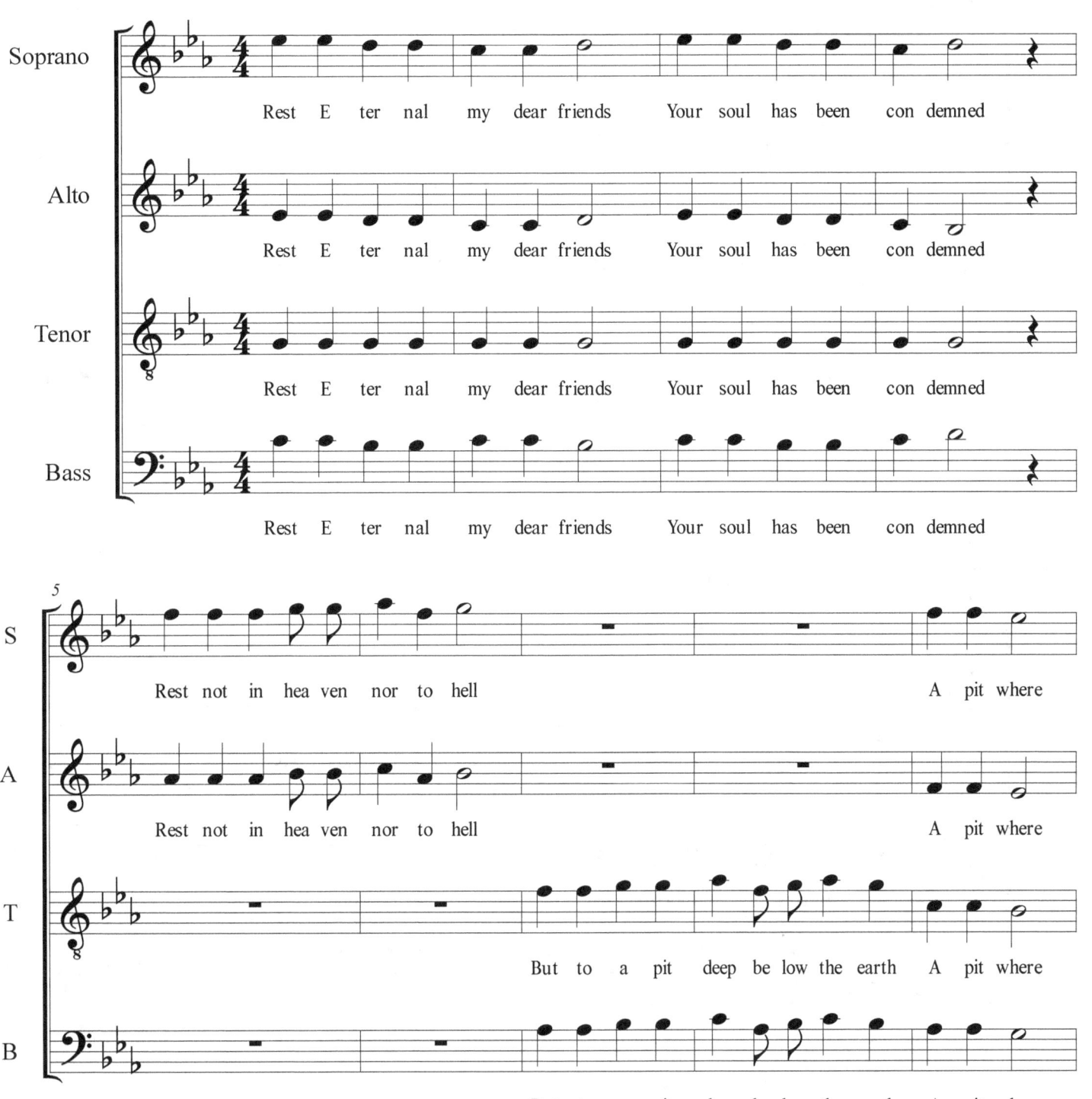

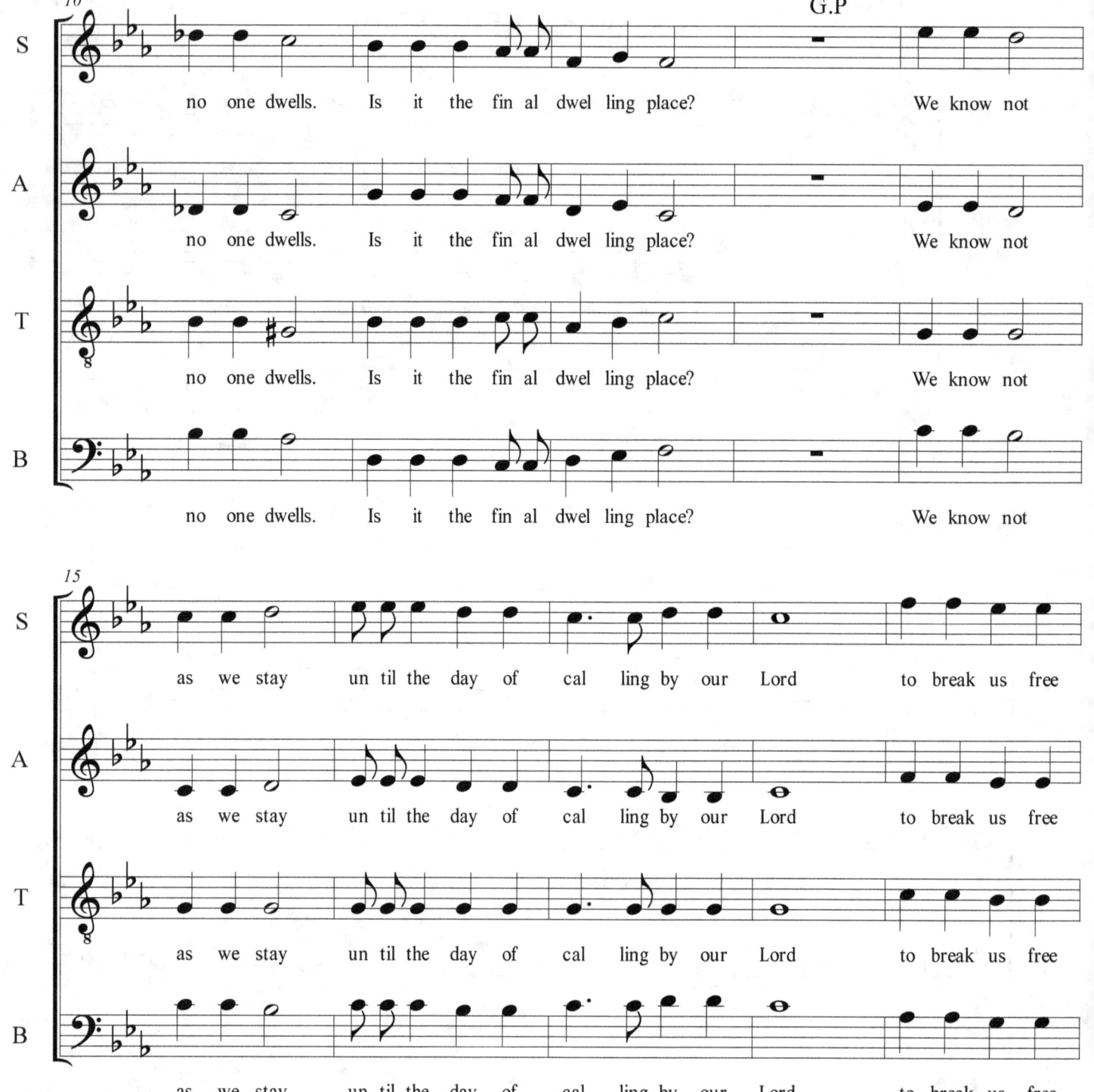

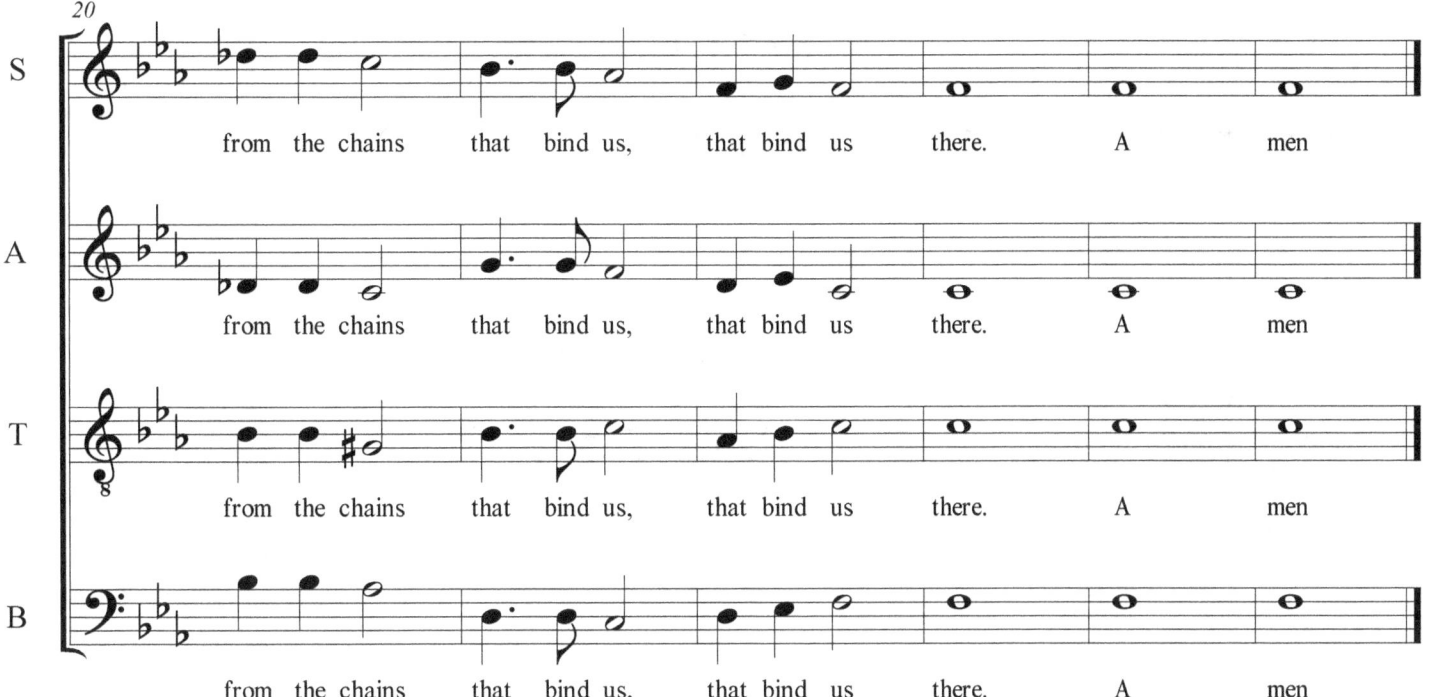

from the chains that bind us, that bind us there. A men

from the chains that bind us, that bind us there. A men

from the chains that bind us, that bind us there. A men

from the chains that bind us, that bind us there. A men

Kyrie Elieson - Have Mercy

Requiem of Lost Souls

Kristina Howells

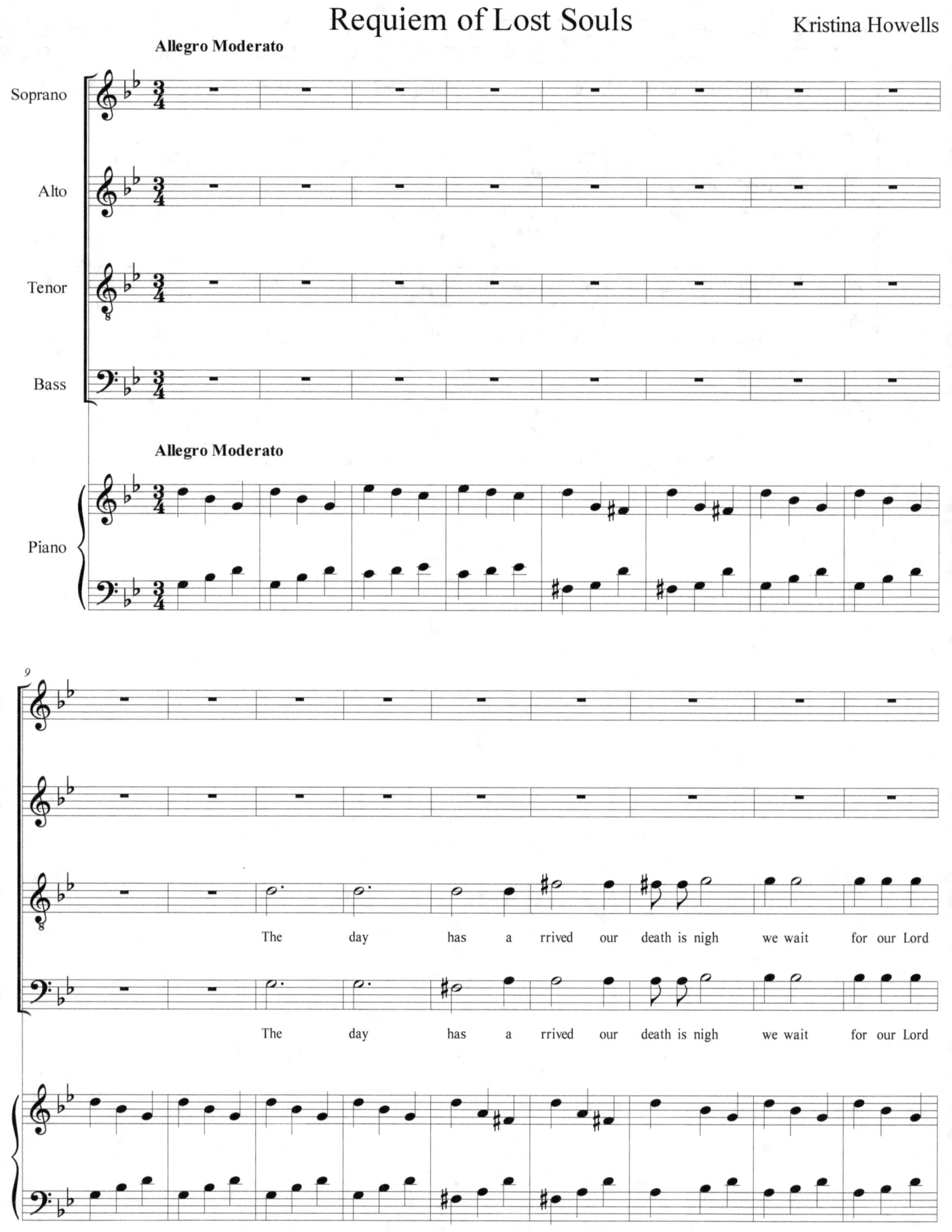

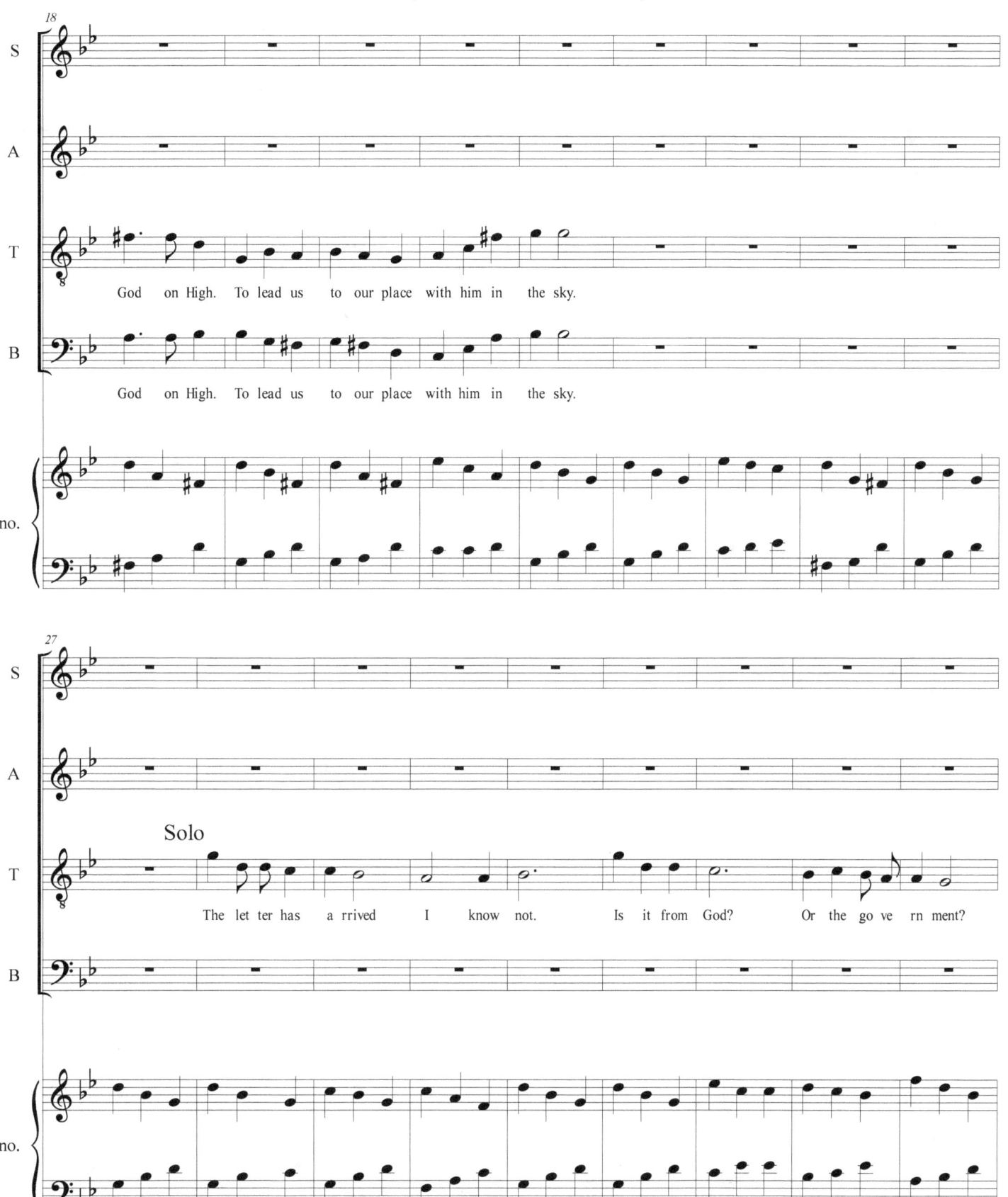

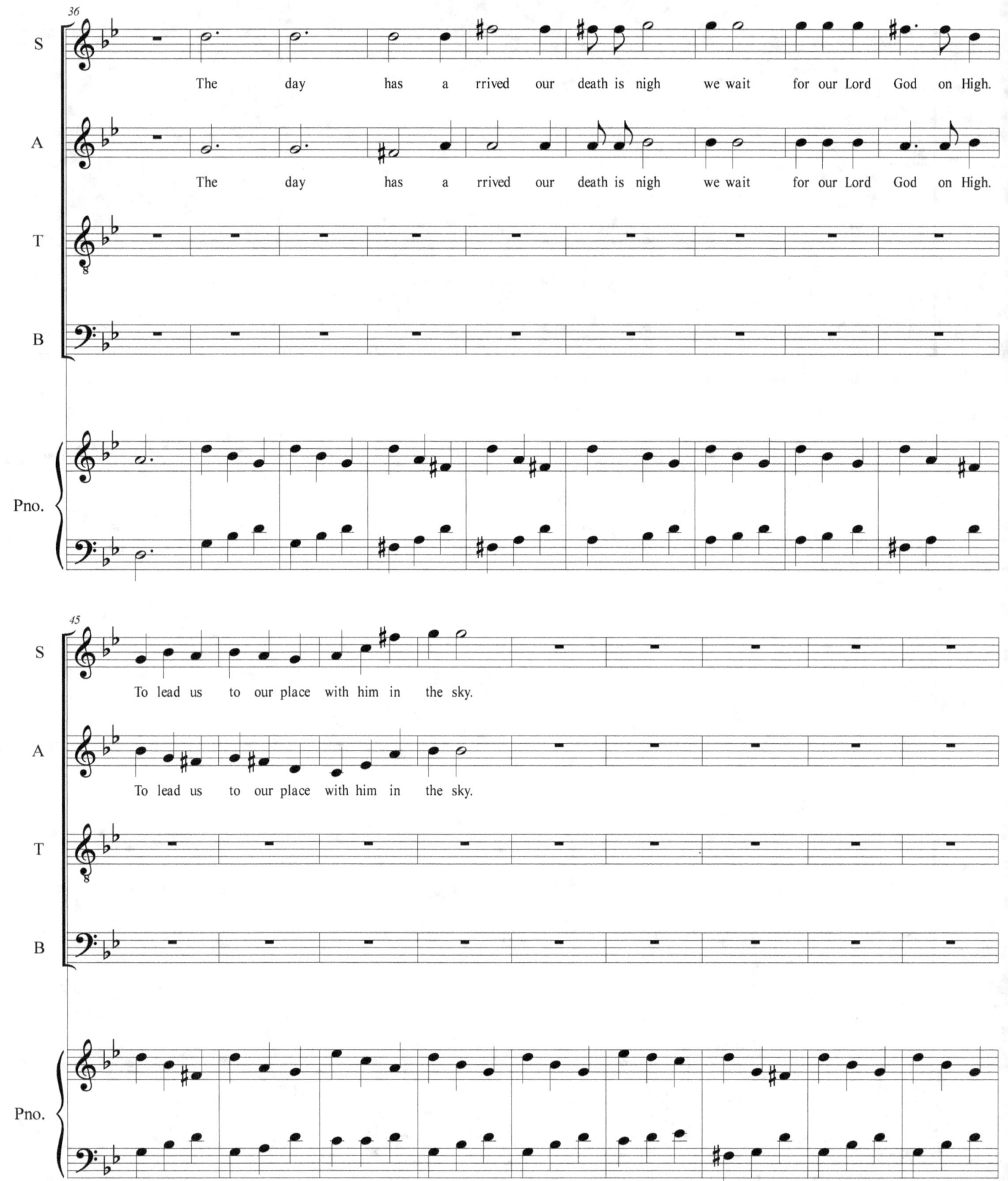

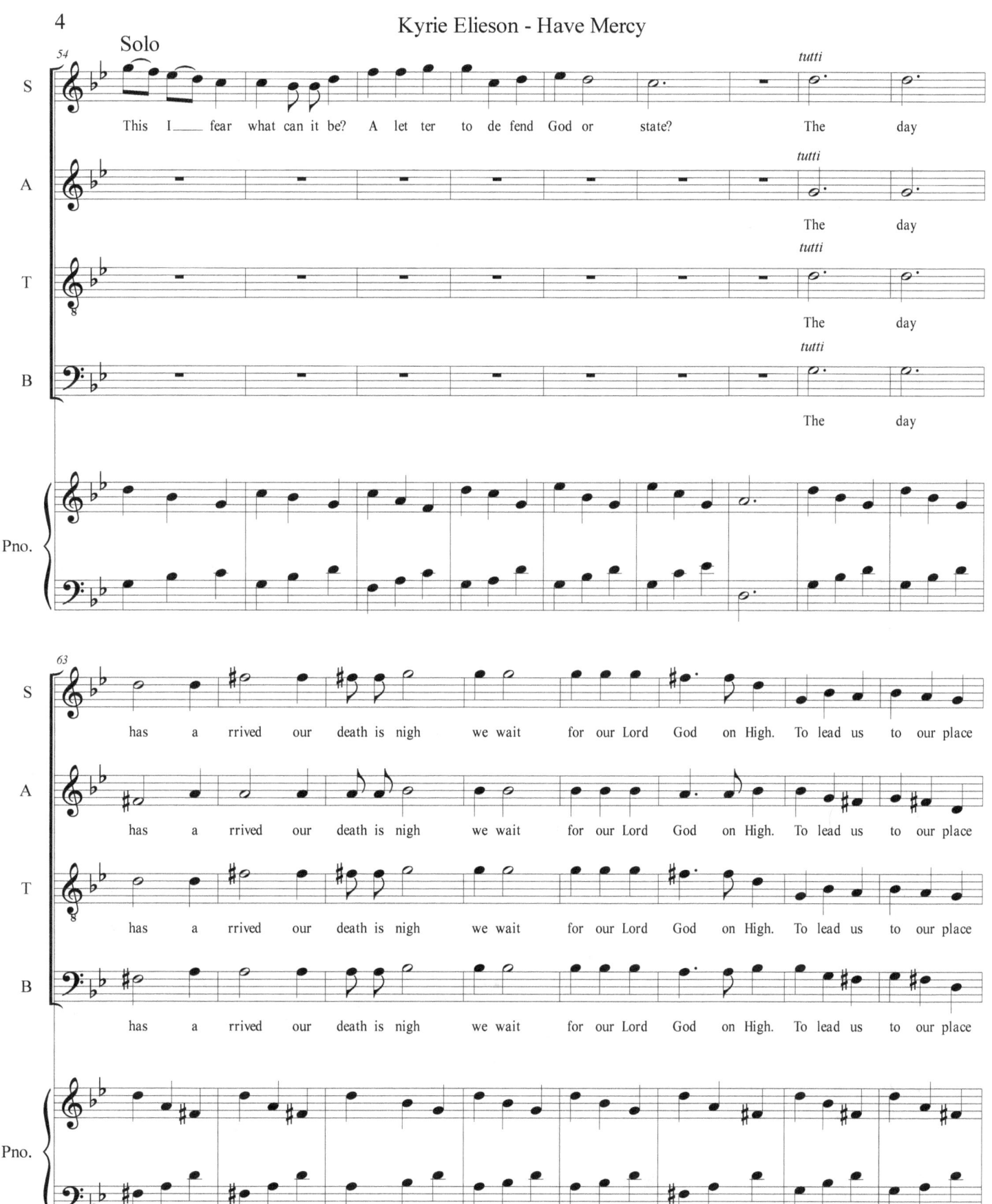

Solo

S: This I____ fear what can it be? A let ter to de fend God or state? The day

A: The day

T: The day

B: The day

S: has a rrived our death is nigh we wait for our Lord God on High. To lead us to our place

A: has a rrived our death is nigh we wait for our Lord God on High. To lead us to our place

T: has a rrived our death is nigh we wait for our Lord God on High. To lead us to our place

B: has a rrived our death is nigh we wait for our Lord God on High. To lead us to our place

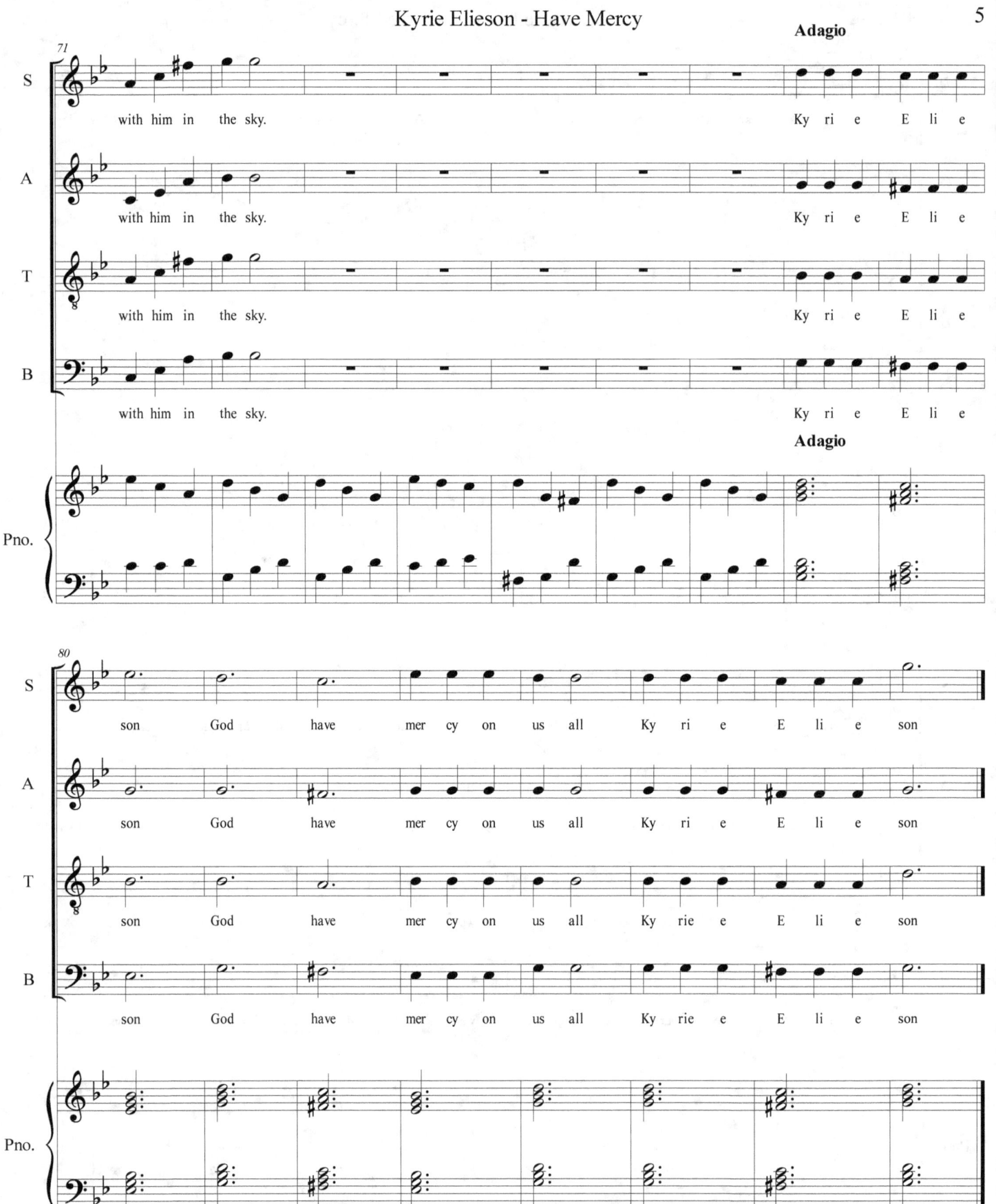

Day of Wrath

Requiem of Lost Souls

Kristina Howells

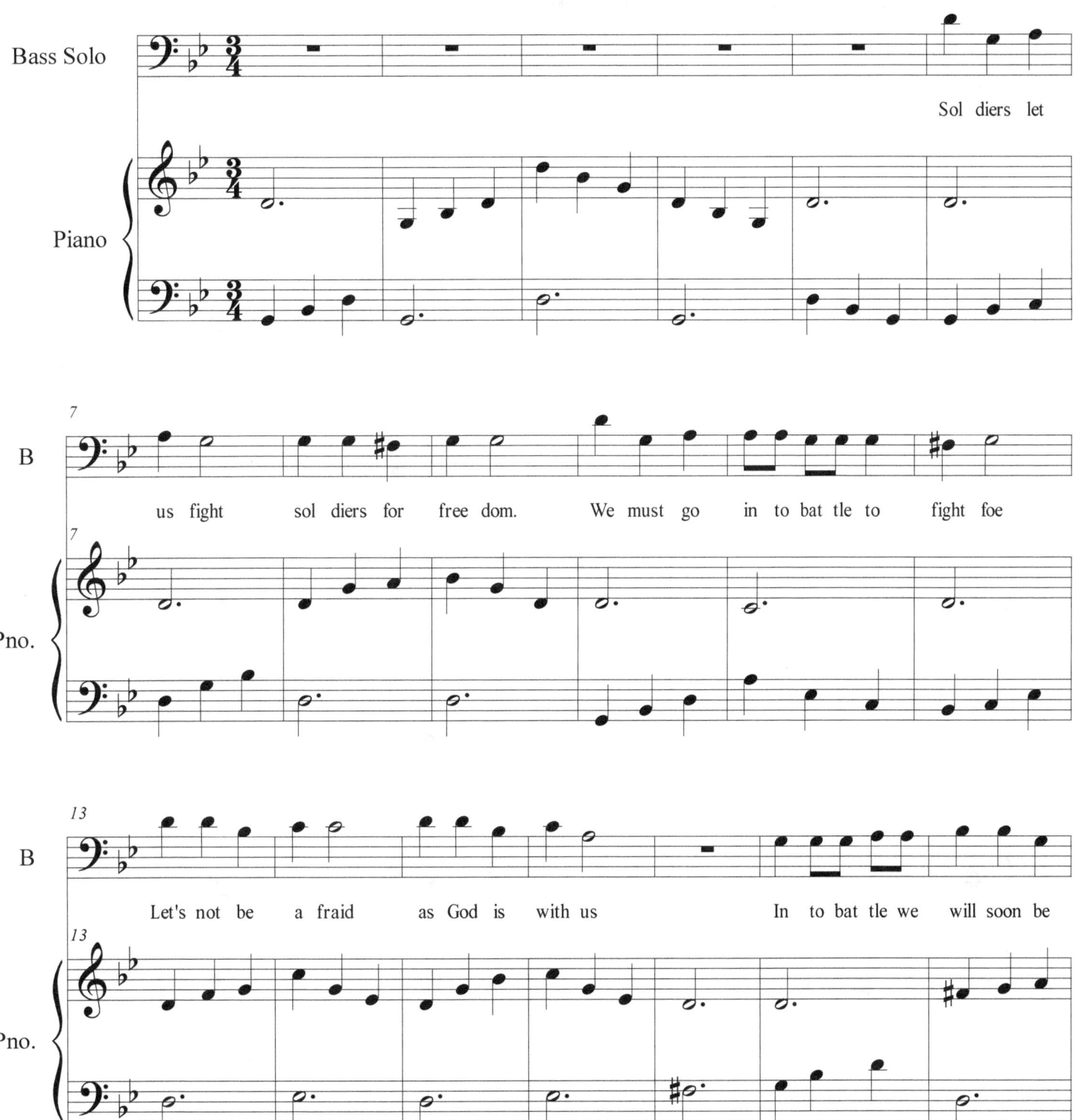

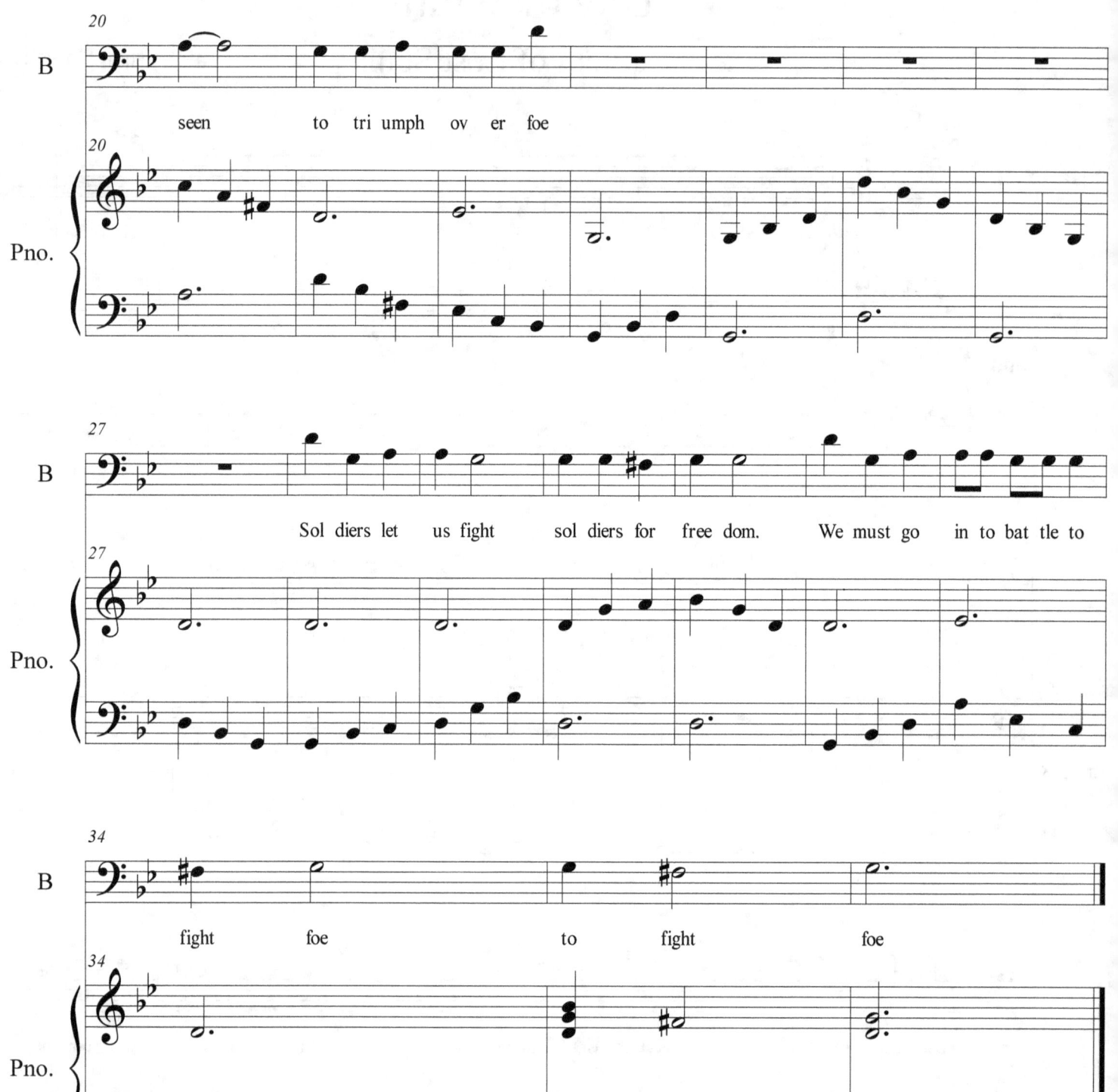

Hark the Trumpets

Requiem of Lost Souls

Kristina Howells

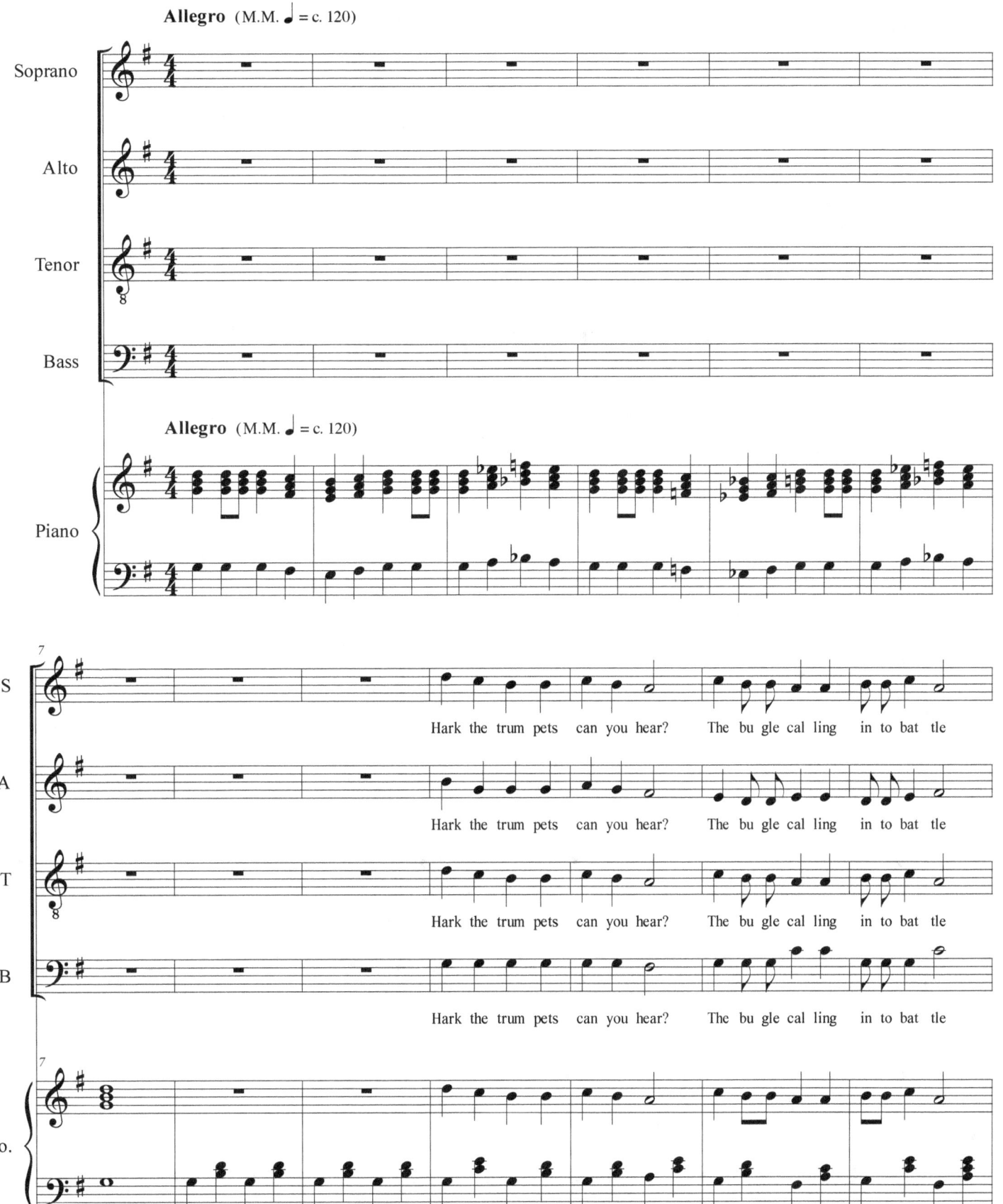

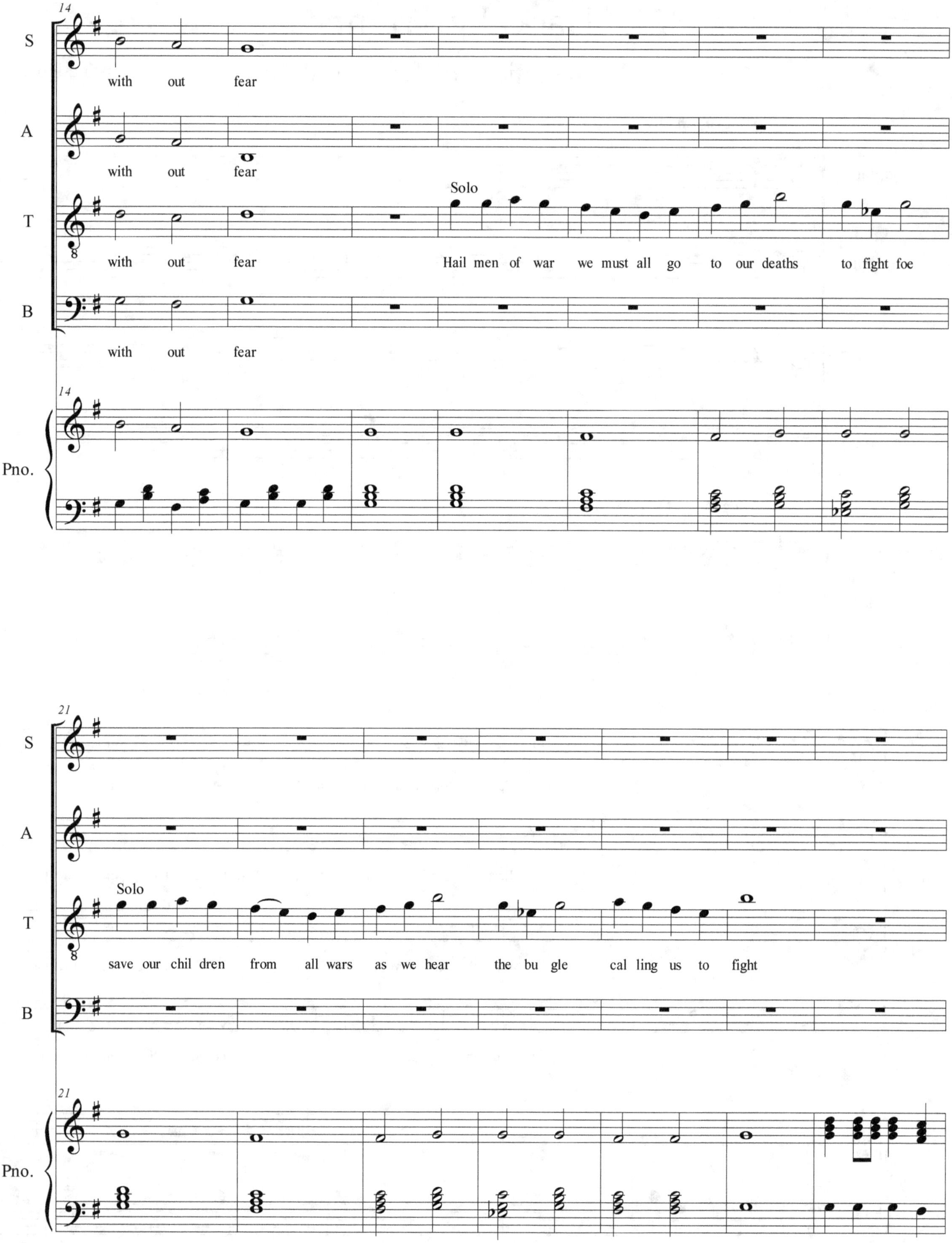

Hark the Trumpets

S: with out fear

A: with out fear

T: with out fear | Solo Hail men of war we must all go to our deaths to fight foe

B: with out fear

T: Solo save our chil dren from all wars as we hear the bu gle cal ling us to fight

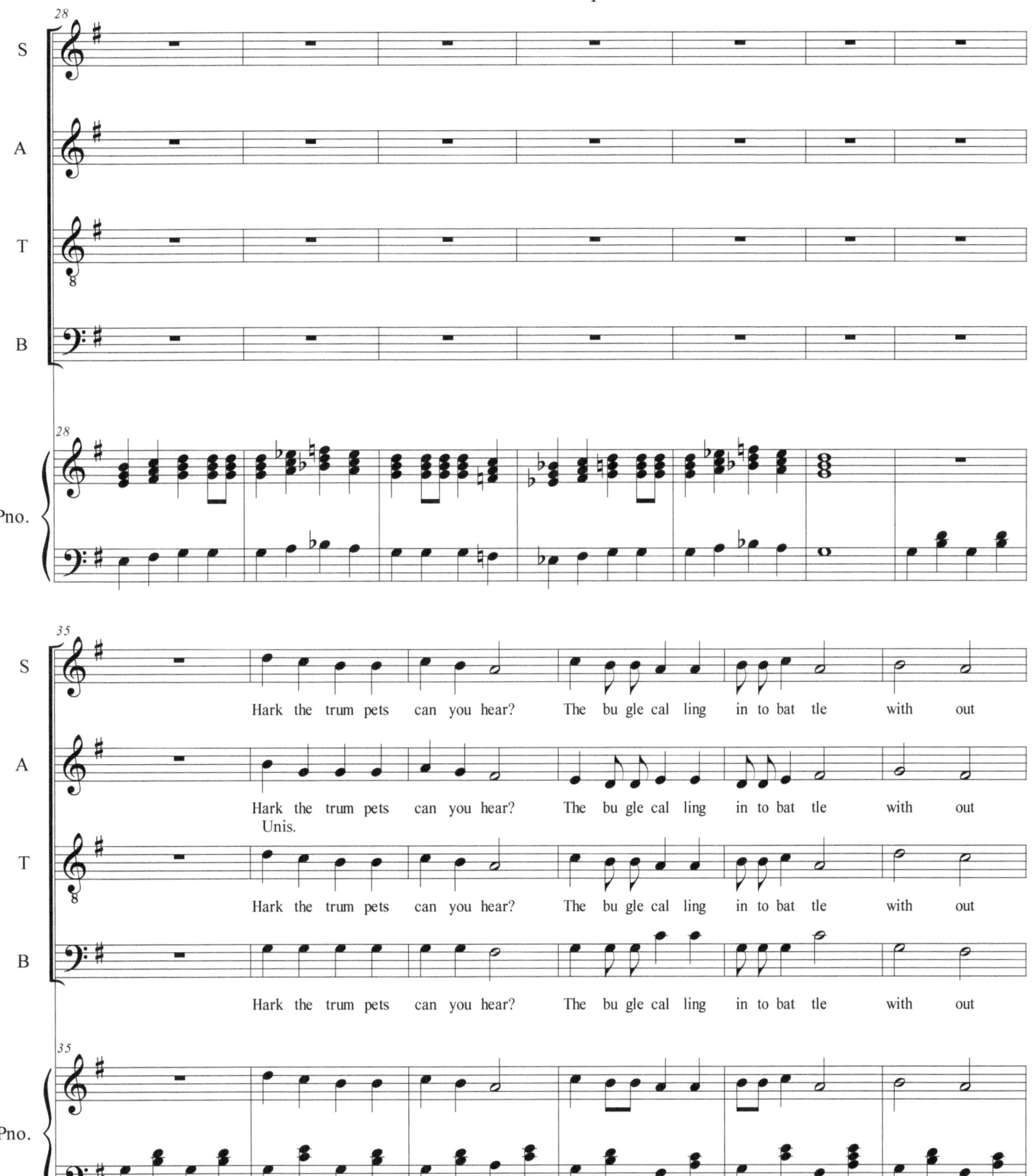

Hark the trum pets can you hear? The bu gle cal ling in to bat tle with out

Hark the Trumpets

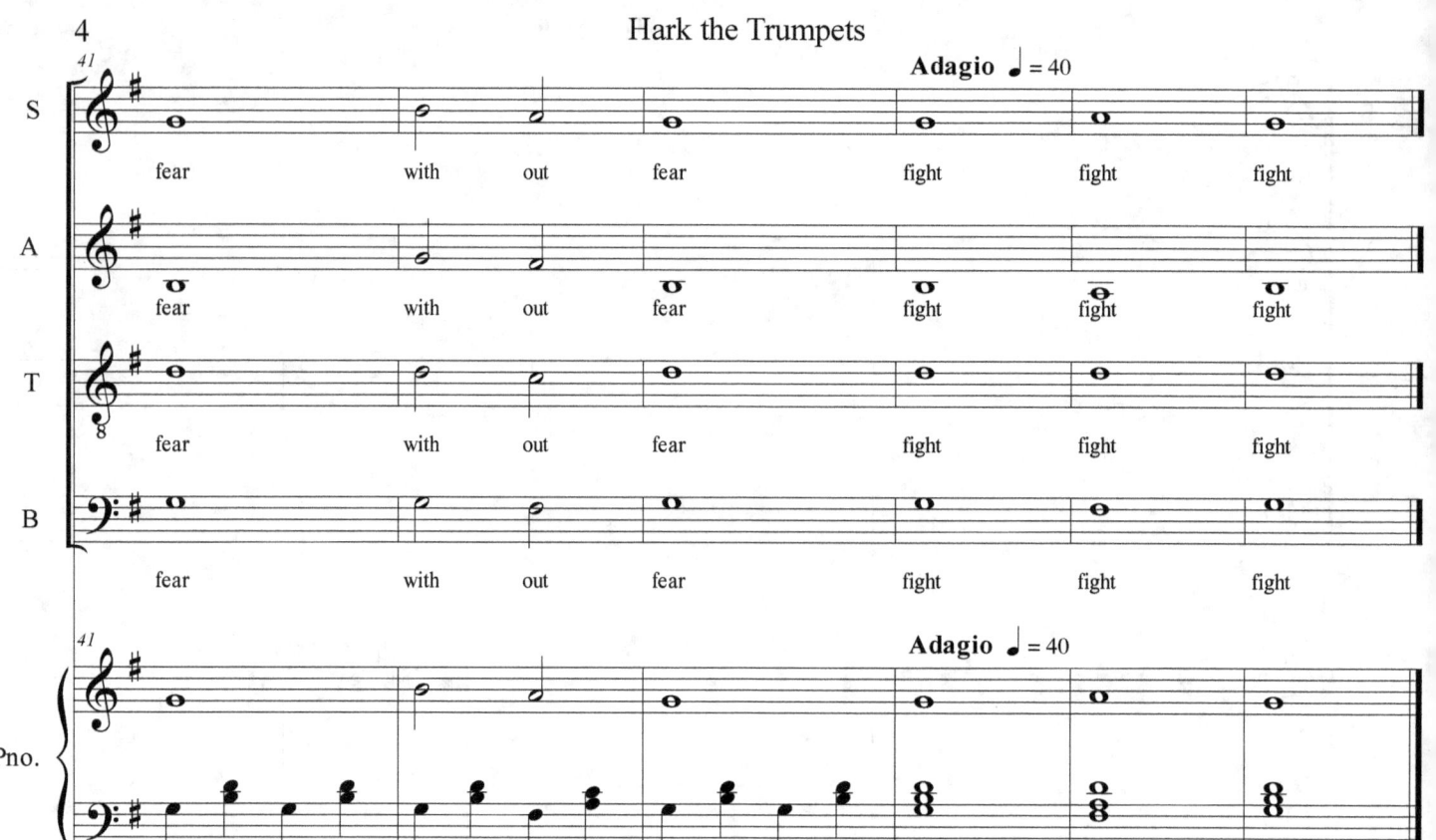

Now the Record

Requiem of Lost Souls

Kristina Howells

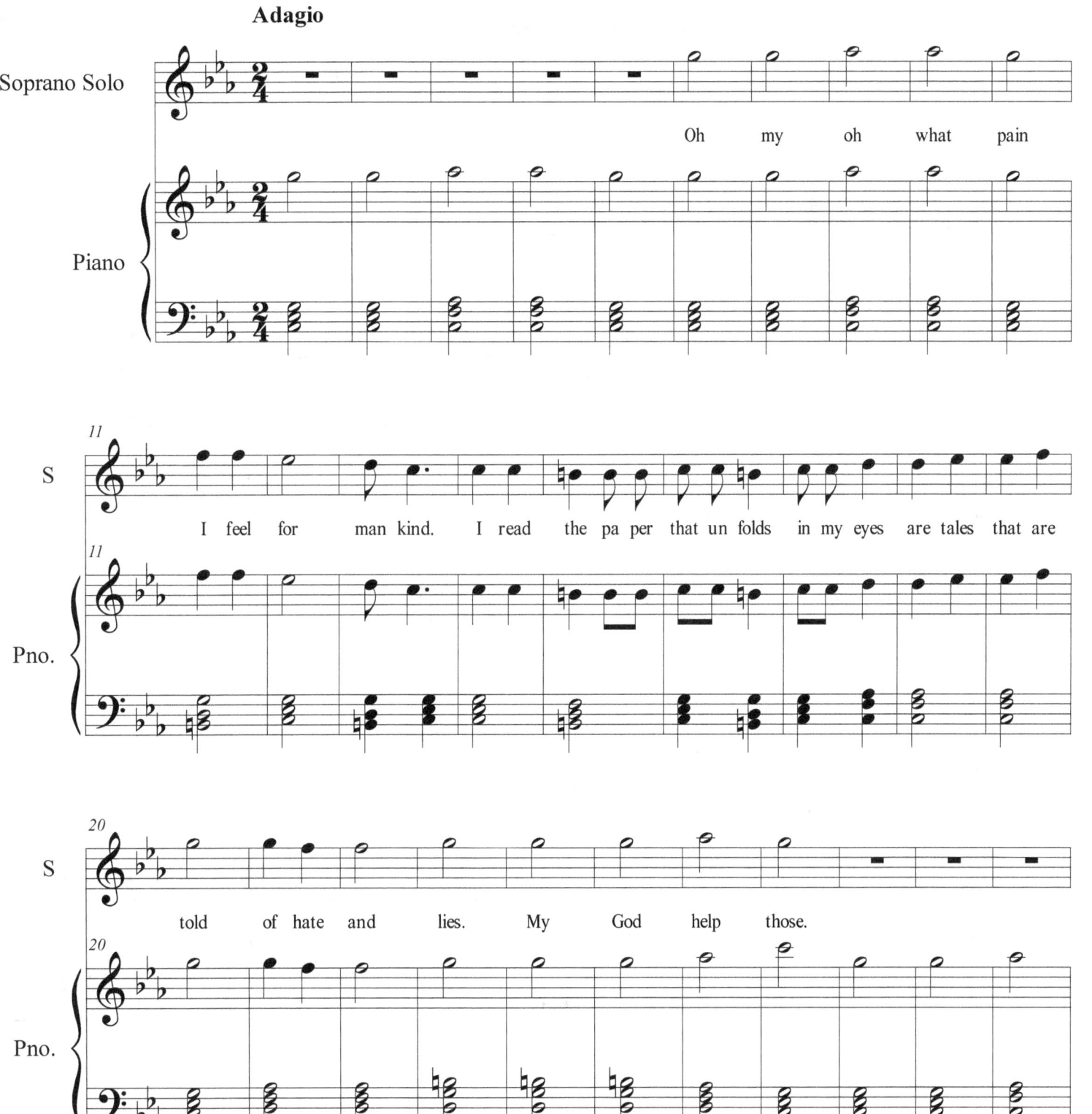

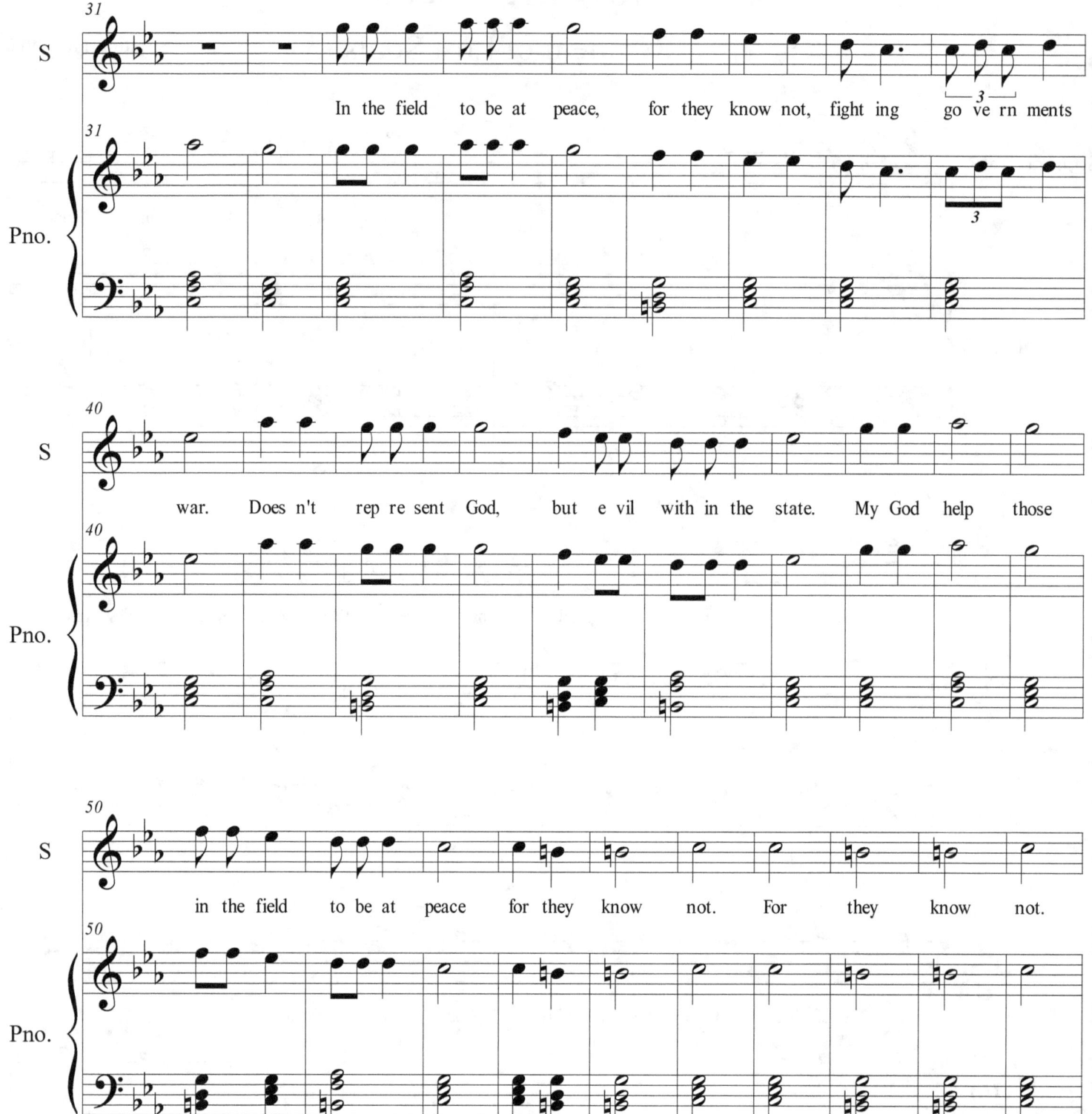

In the field   to be at   peace,   for they know not, fight ing   go ve rn ments

war.   Does n't   rep re sent   God,   but e vil   with in the   state.   My God   help   those

in the field   to be at   peace   for they   know   not.   For   they   know   not.

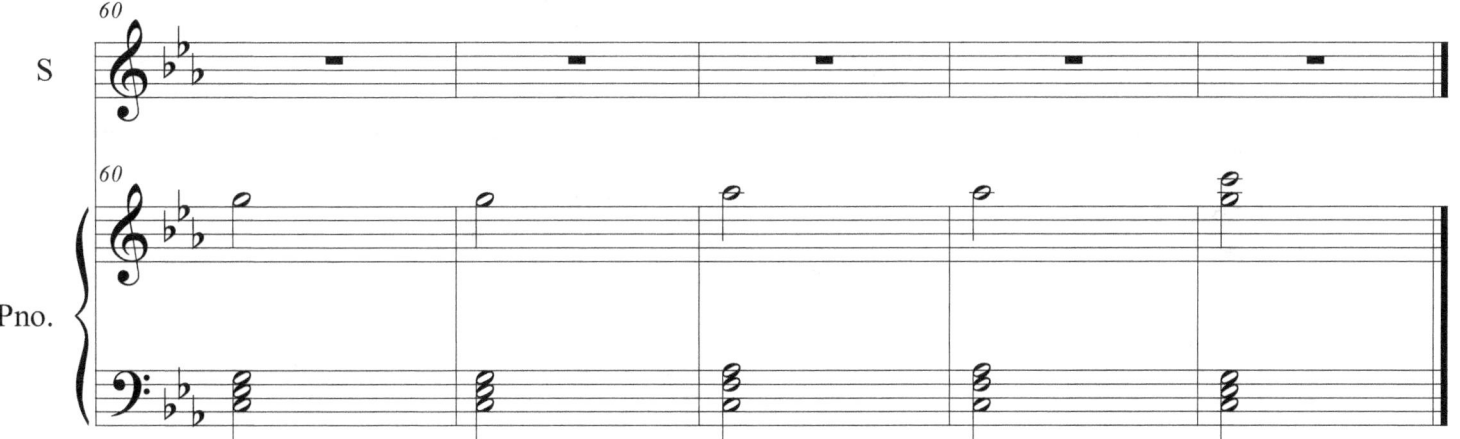

What Affliction?
Requiem of Lost Souls

Kristina Howells

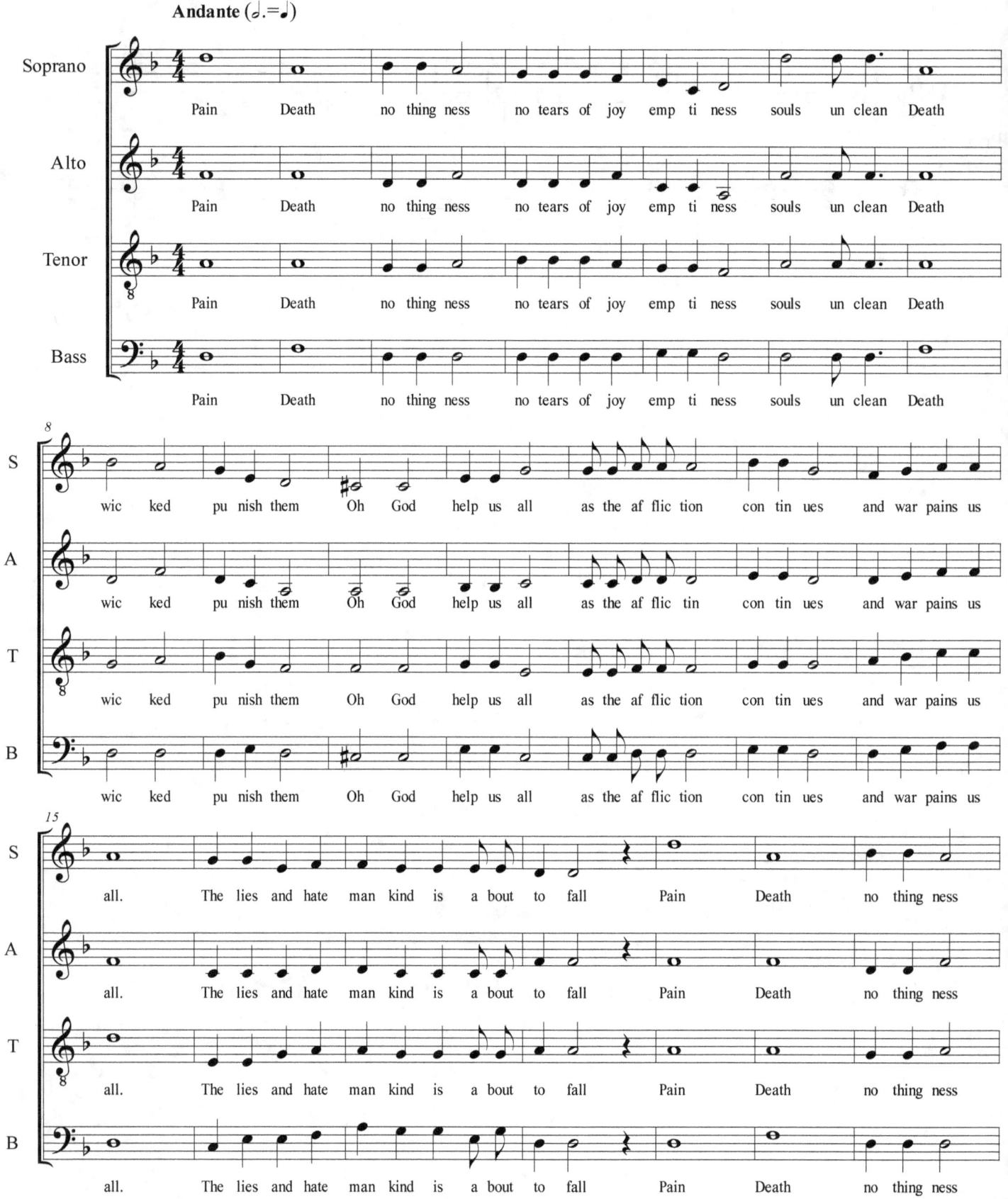

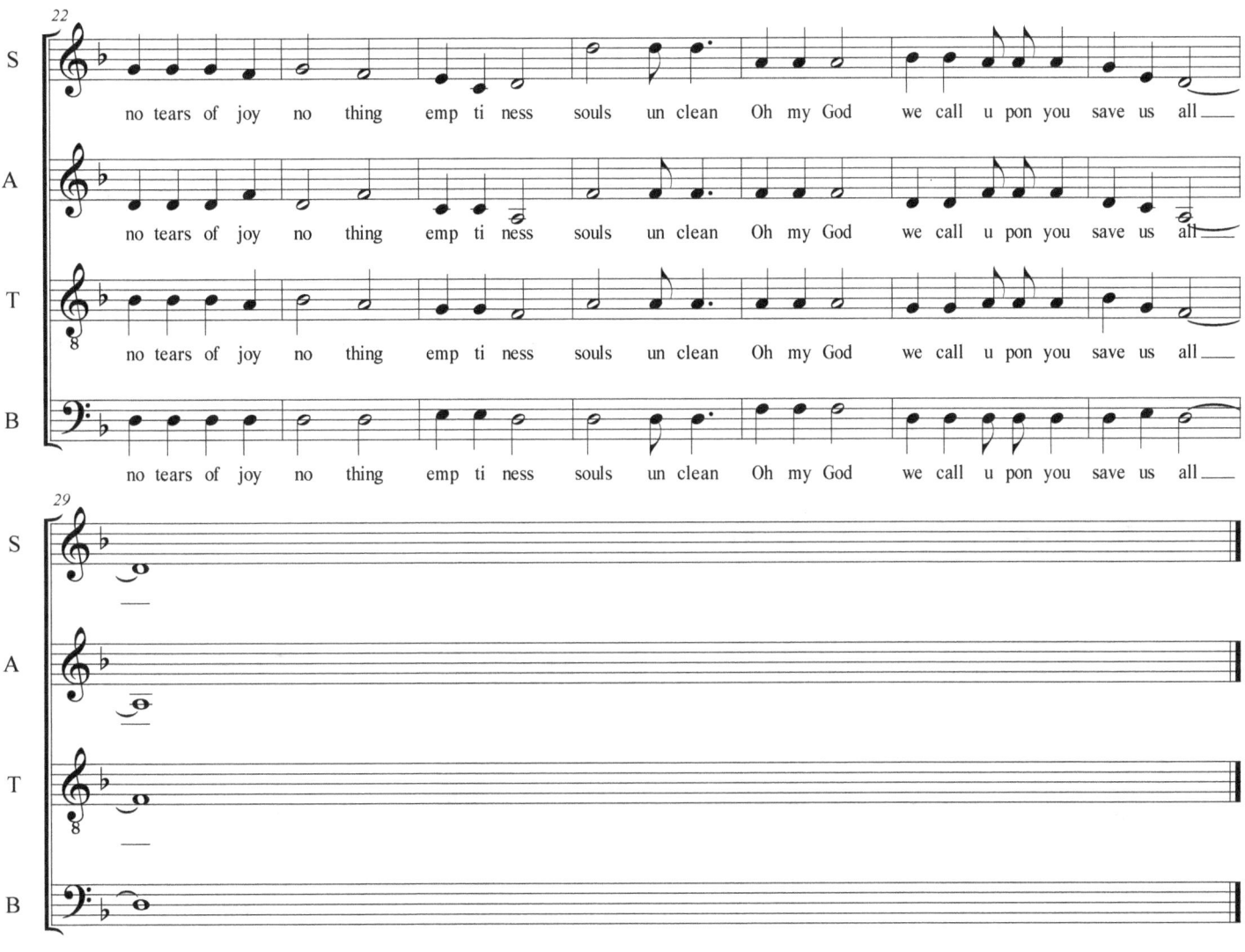

Messenger of God
Requiem of Lost Souls

Kristina Howells

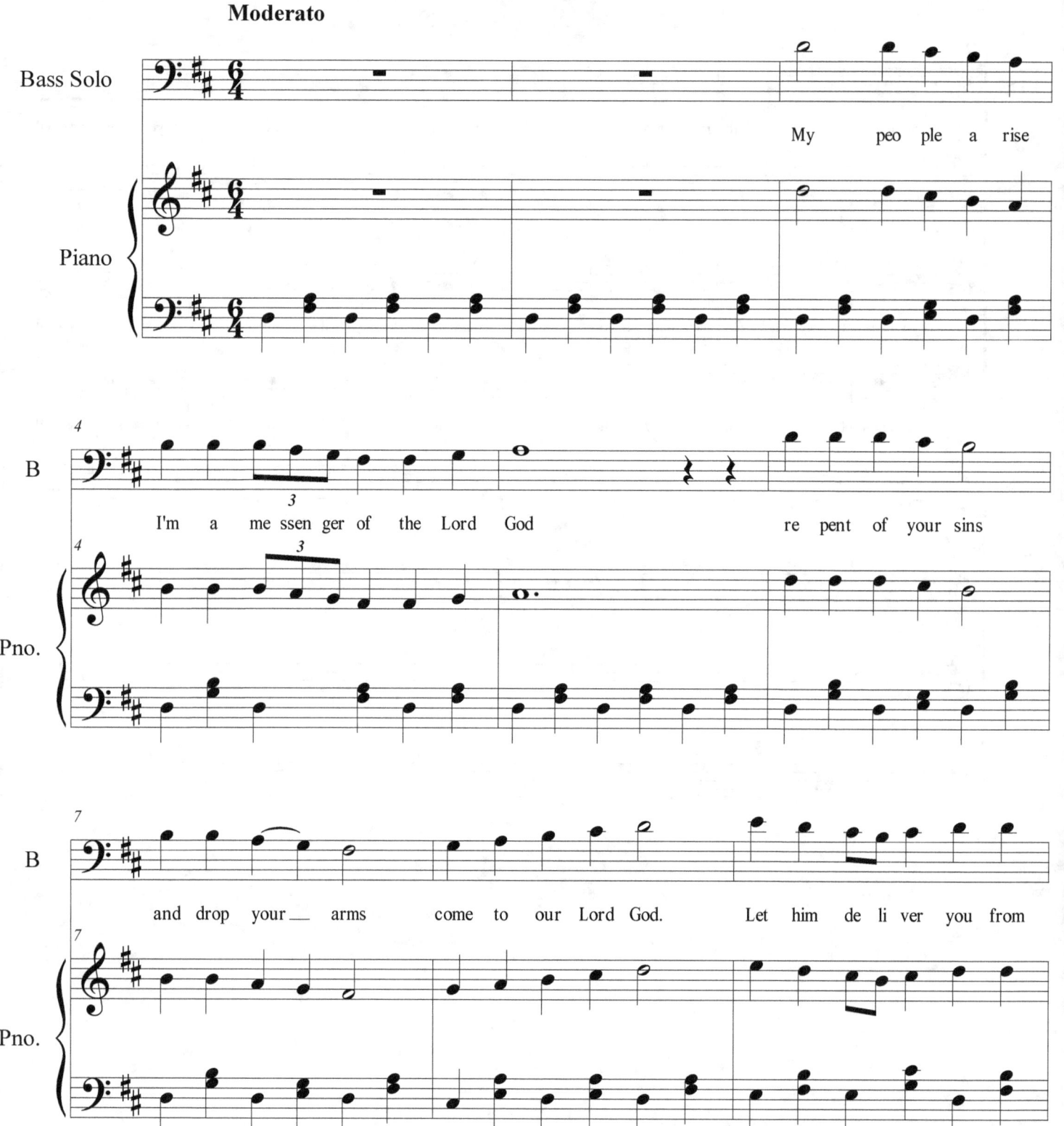

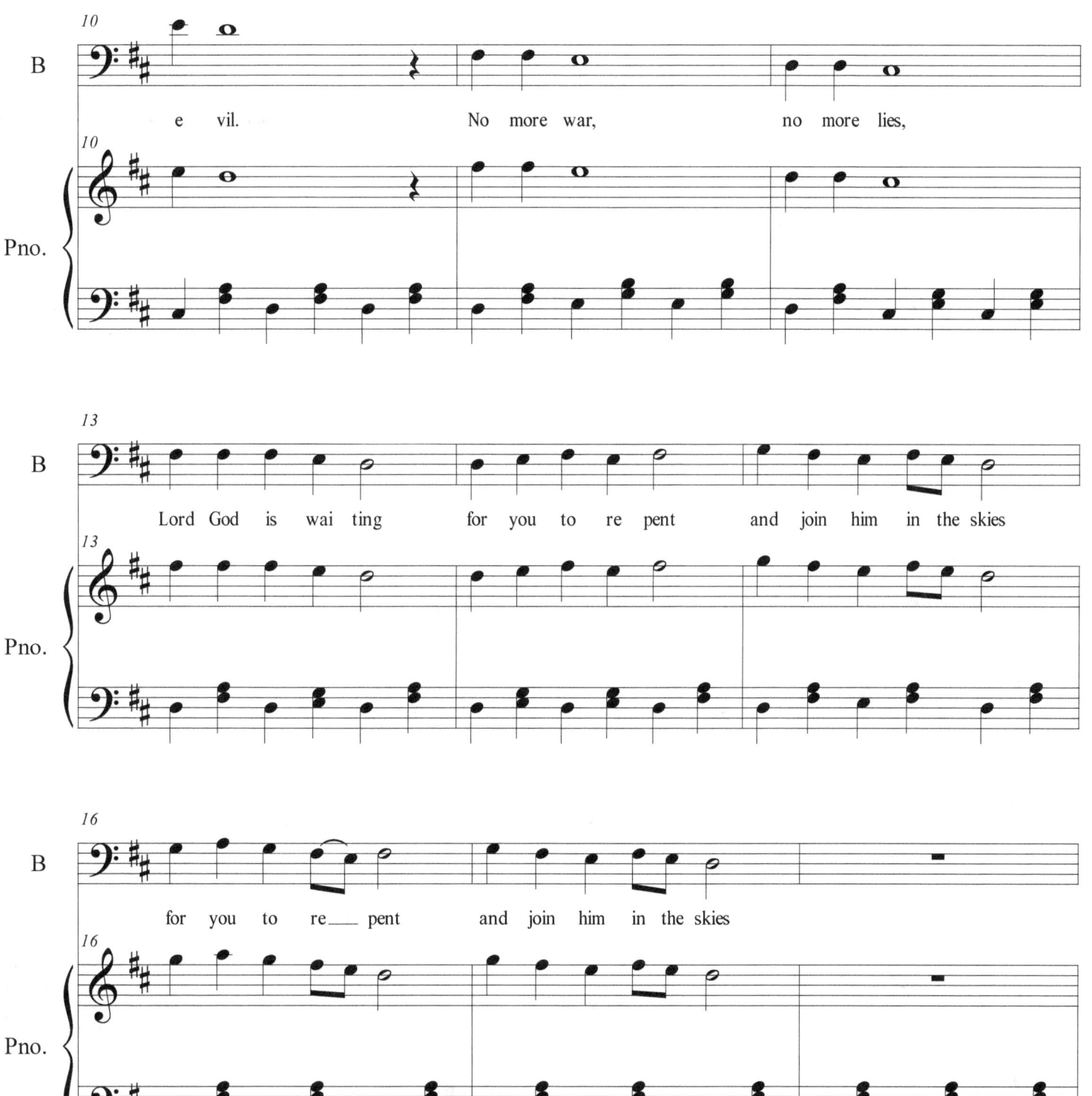

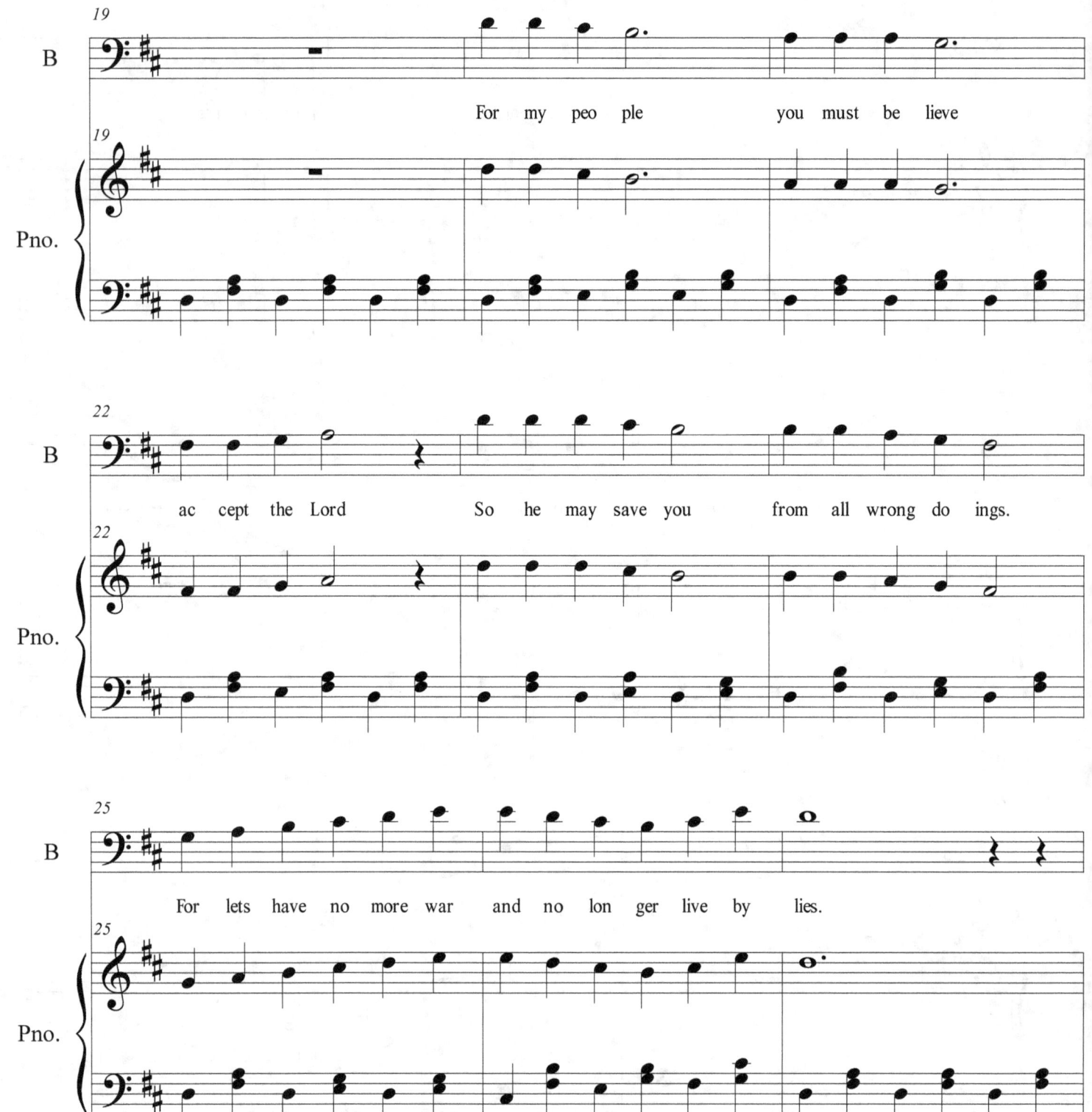

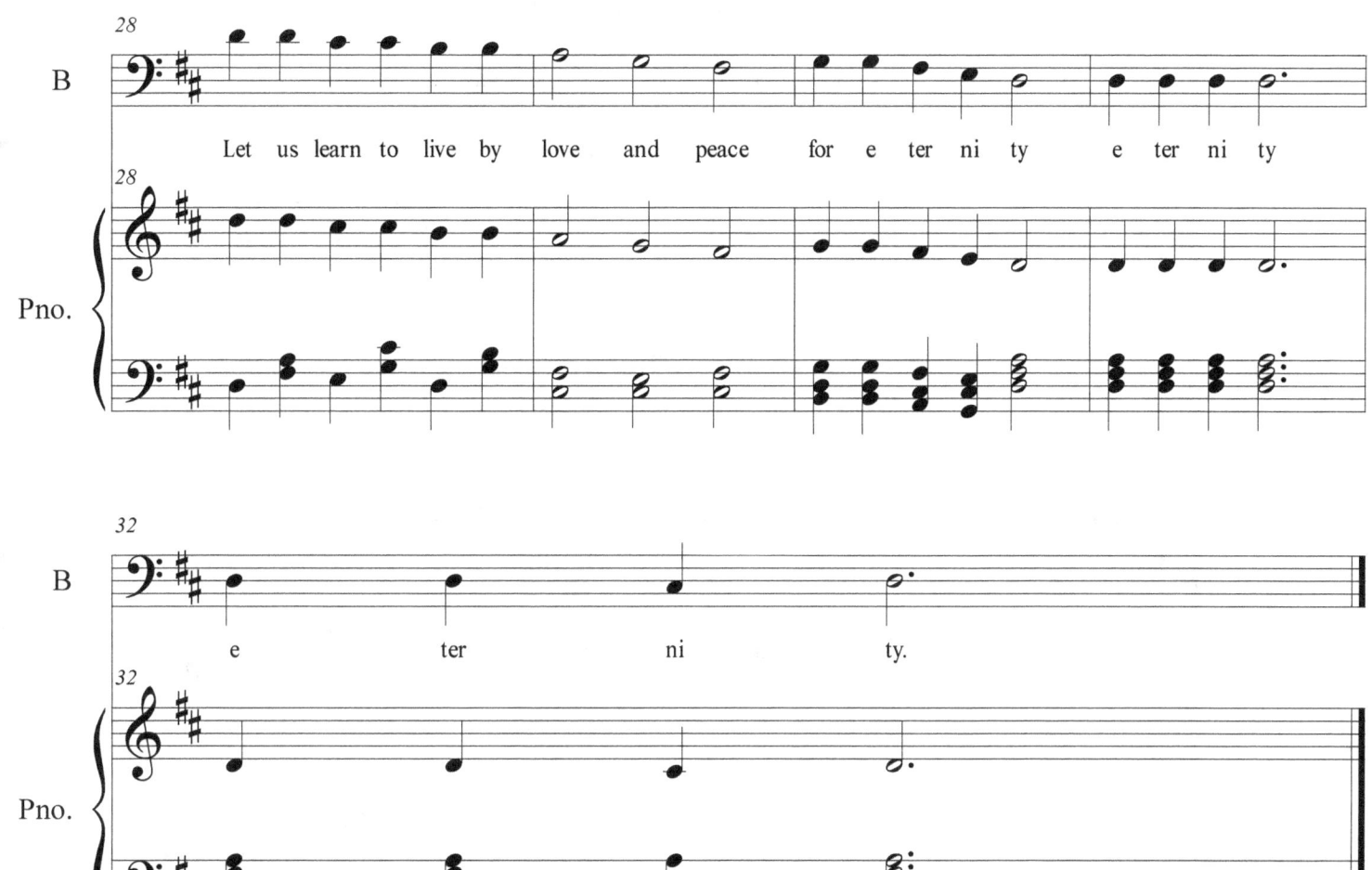

Let us learn to live by love and peace for e ter ni ty e ter ni ty

e ter ni ty.

Remember
Requiem of Lost Souls

Kristina Howells

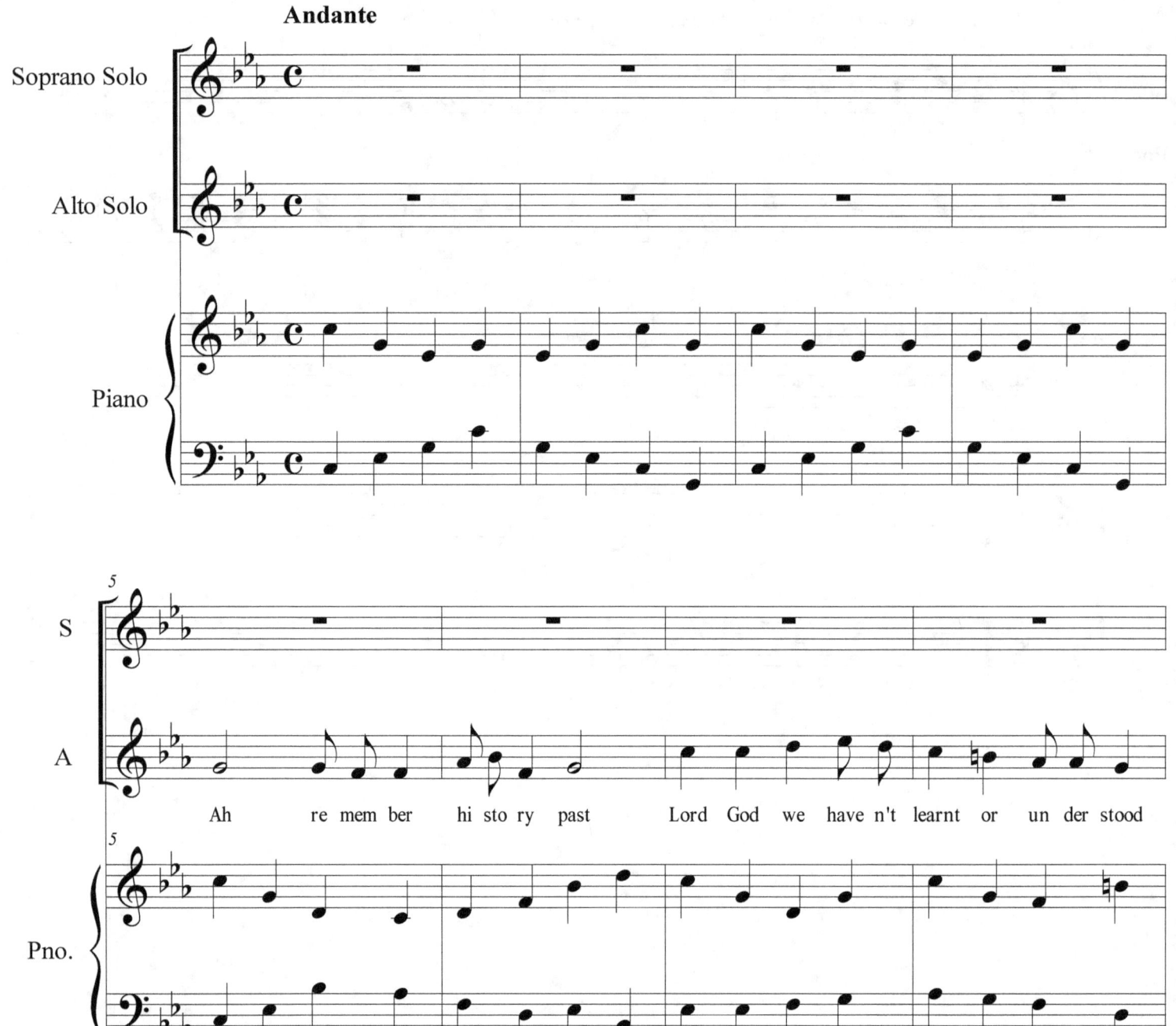

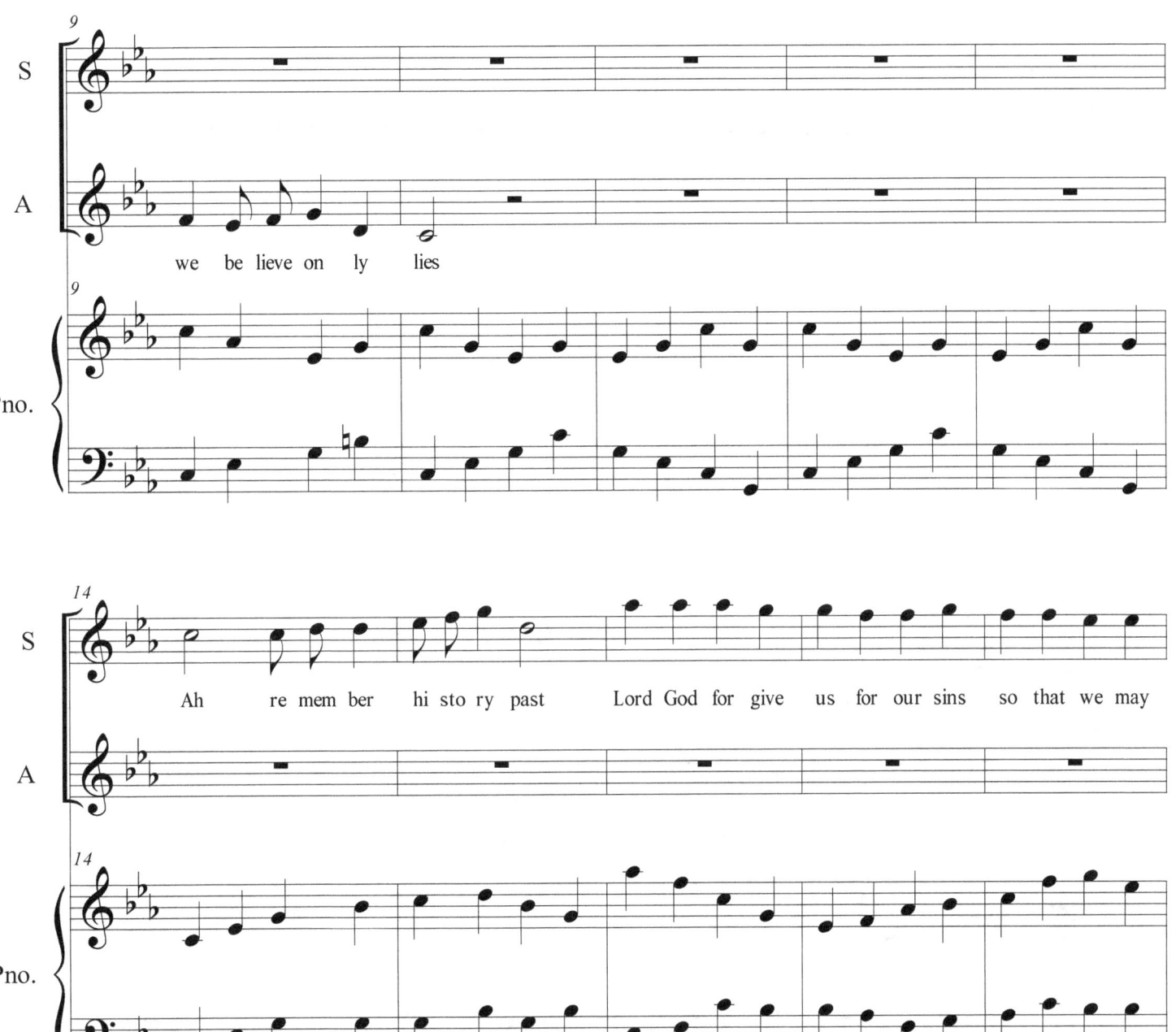

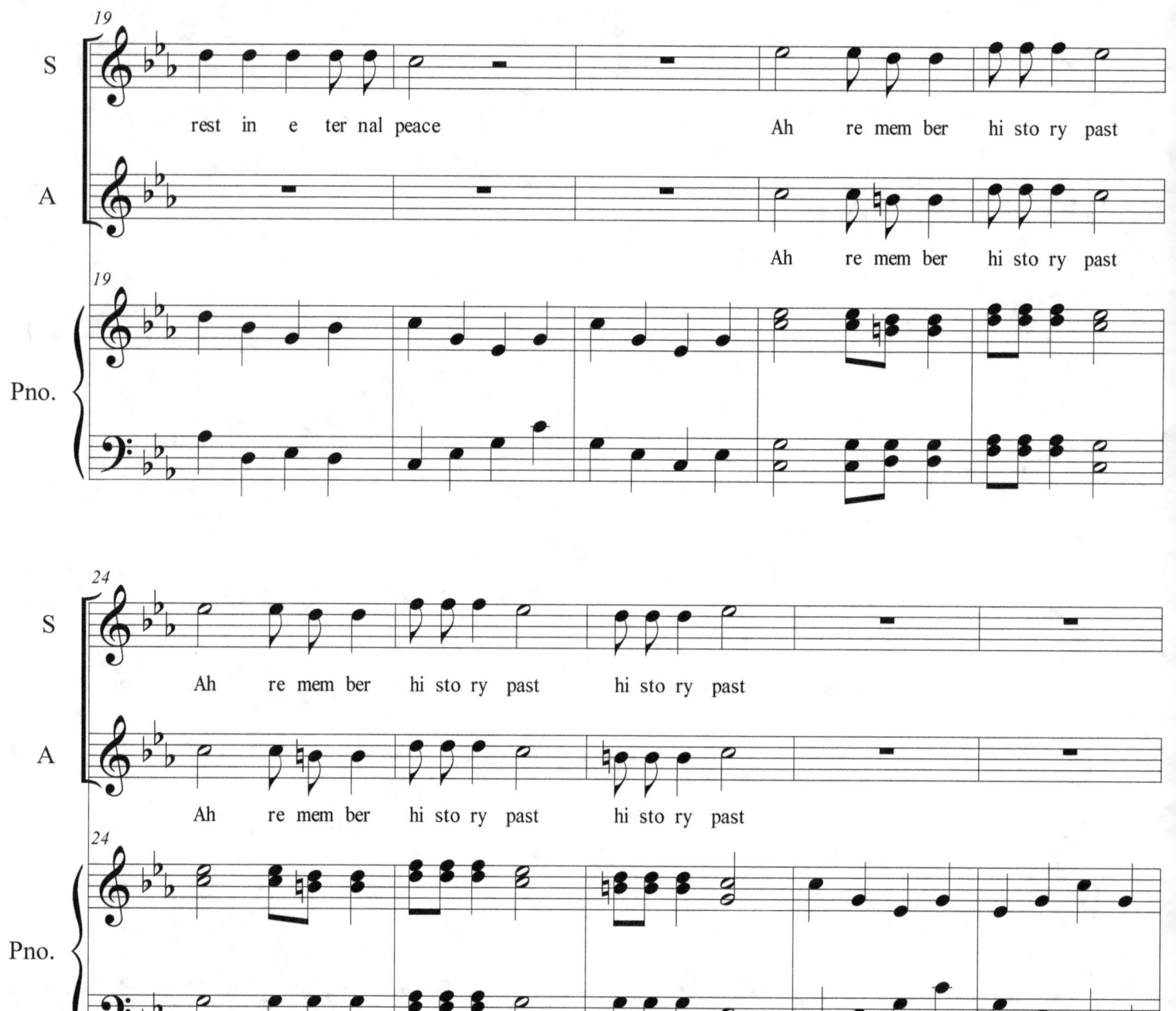

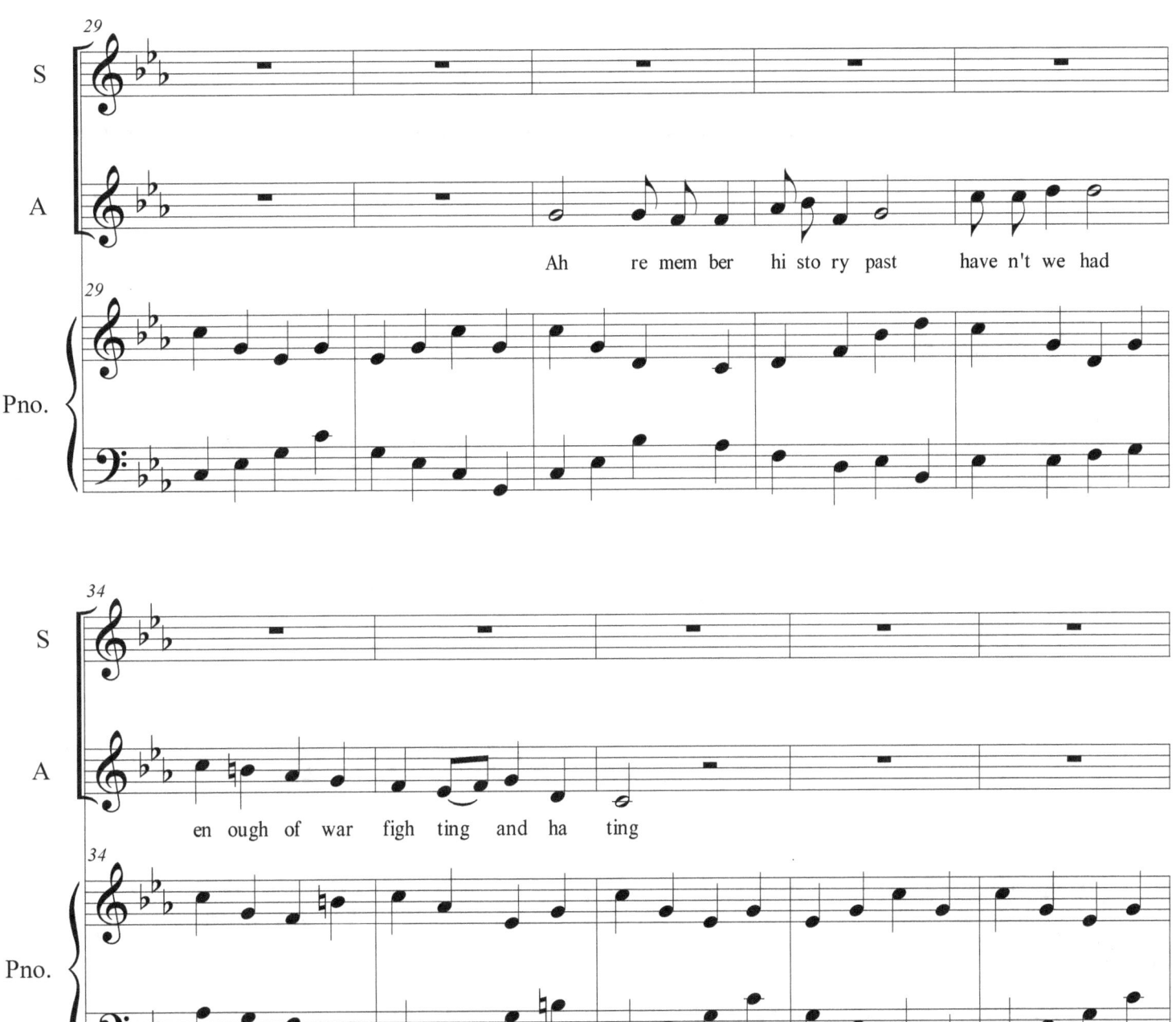

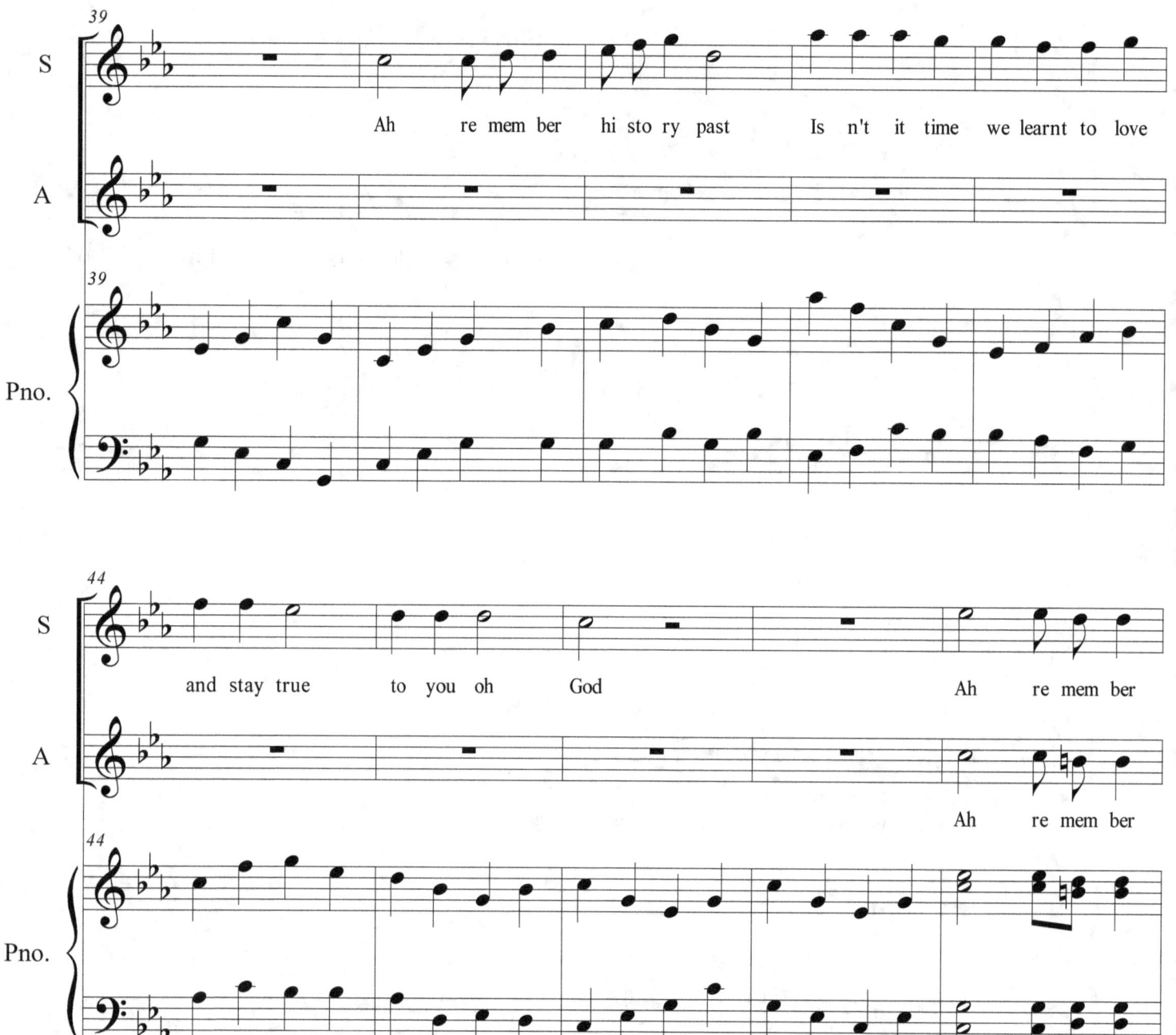

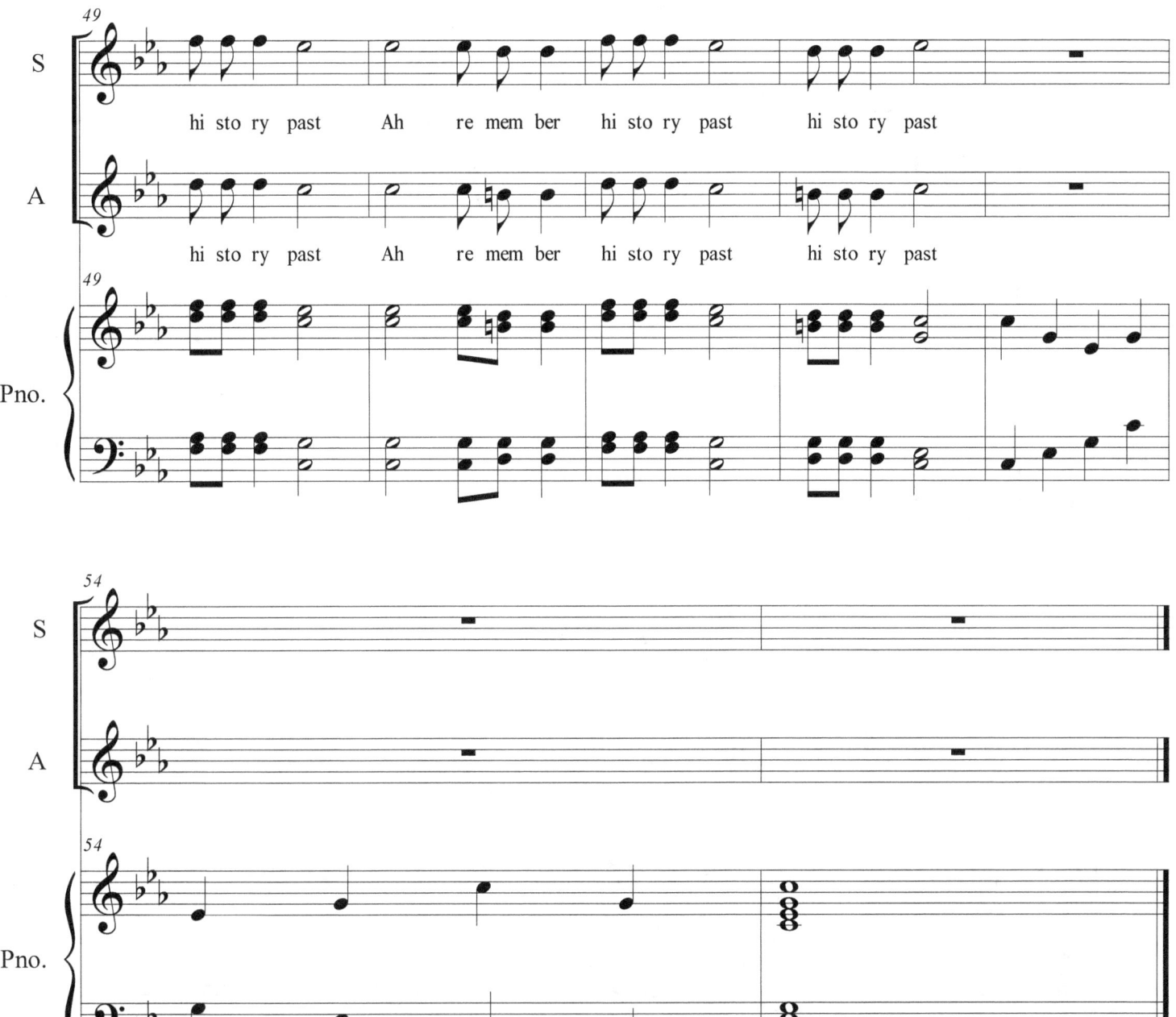

hi sto ry past   Ah   re mem ber   hi sto ry past   hi sto ry past

hi sto ry past   Ah   re mem ber   hi sto ry past   hi sto ry past

Offertorium
Requiem of Lost Souls

Kristina Howells

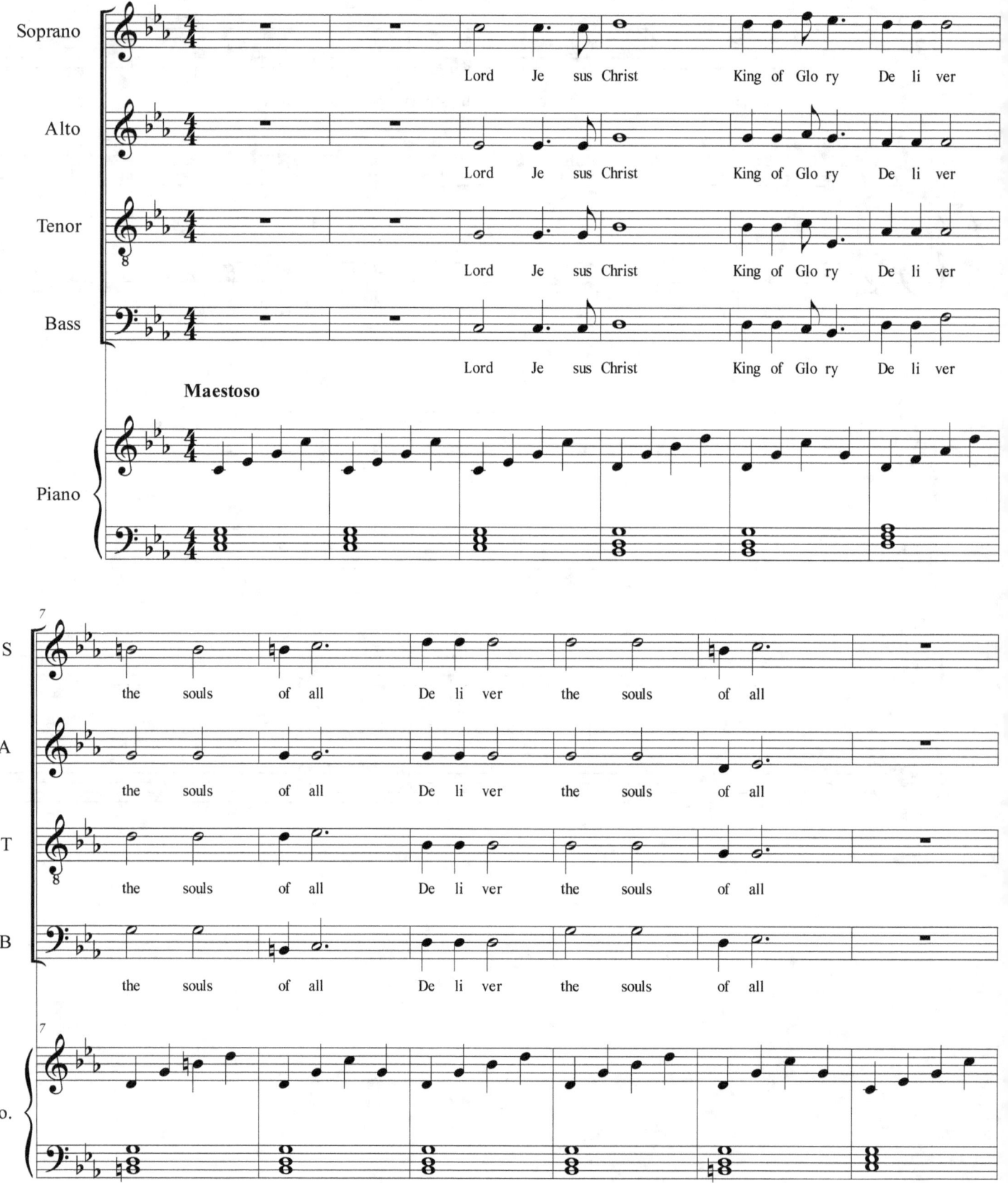

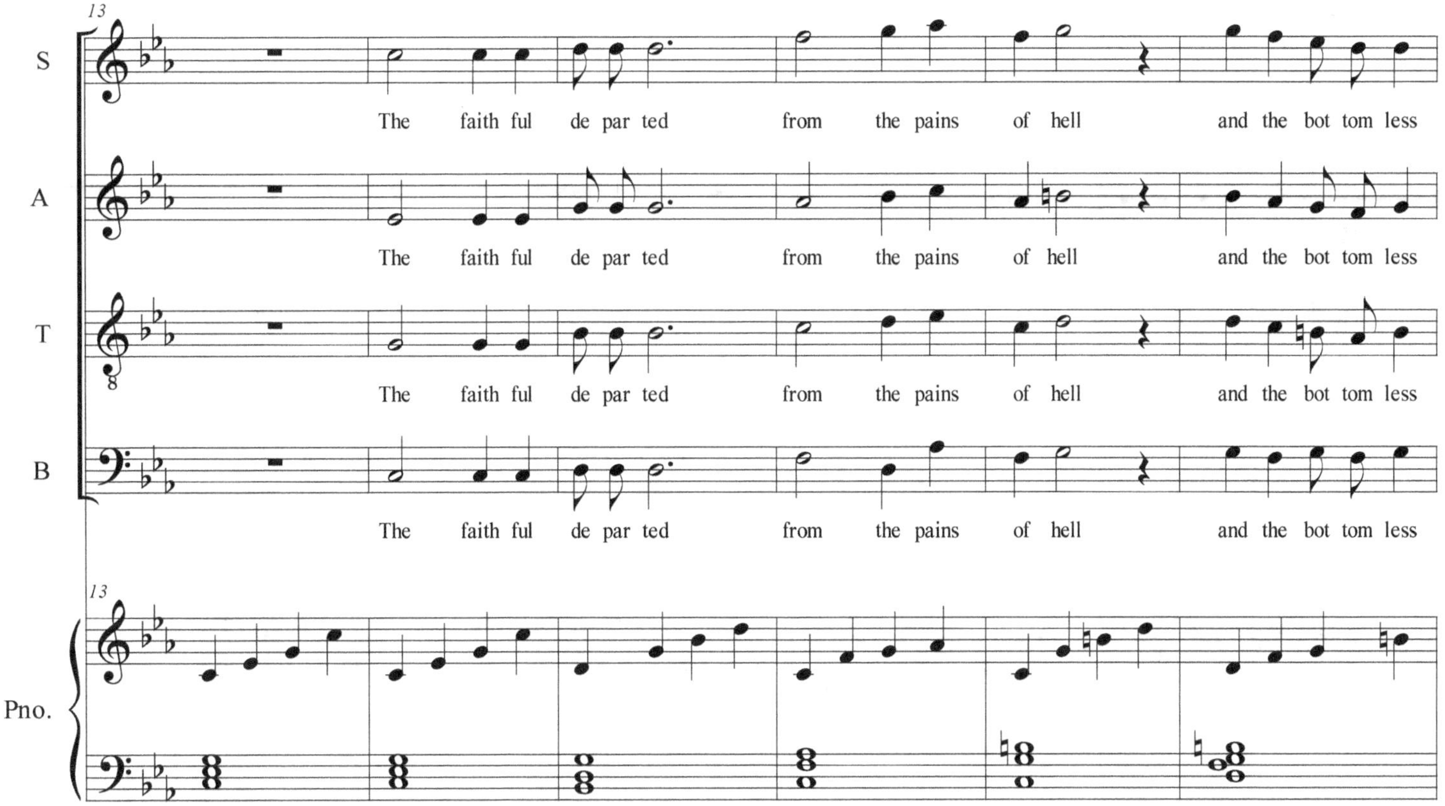

Offertorium

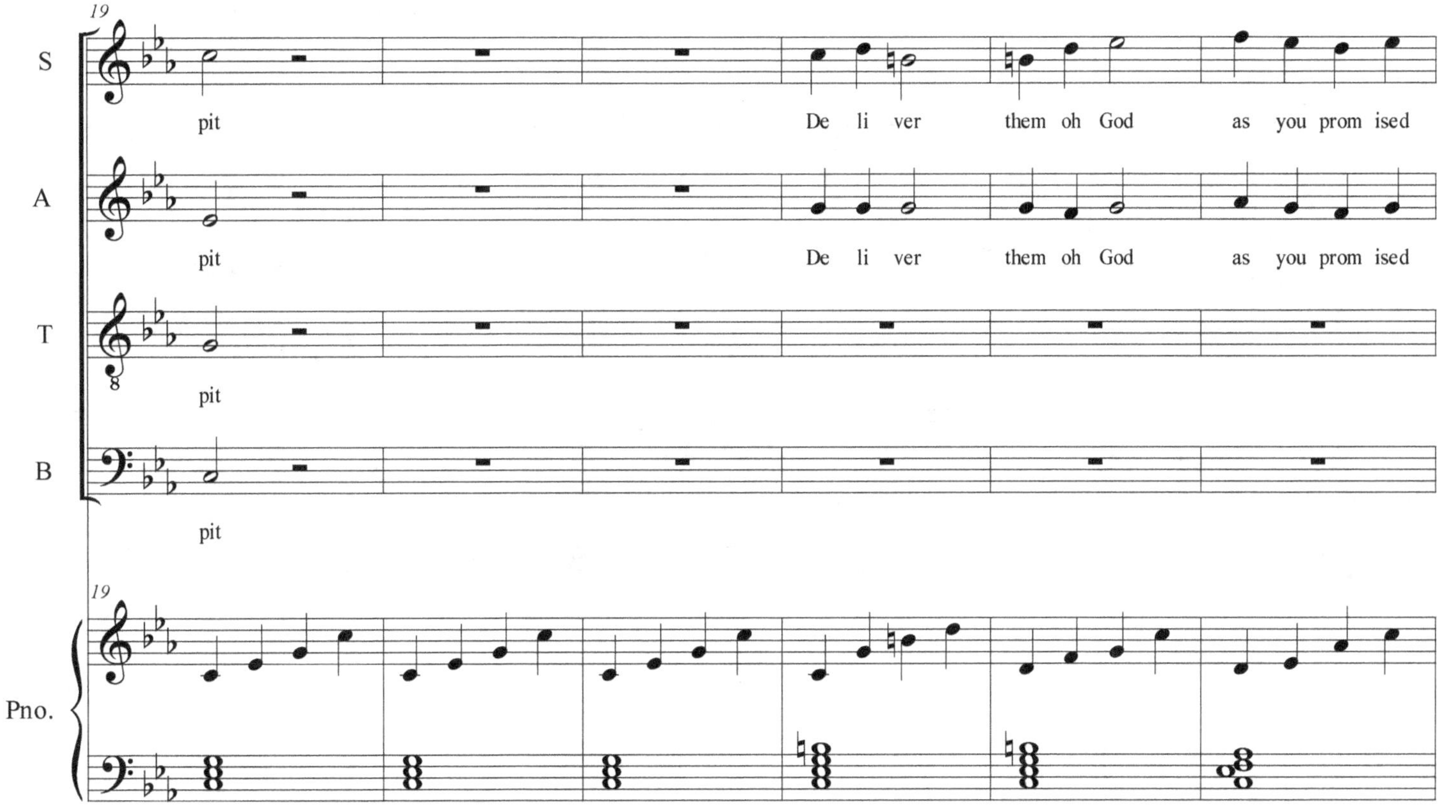

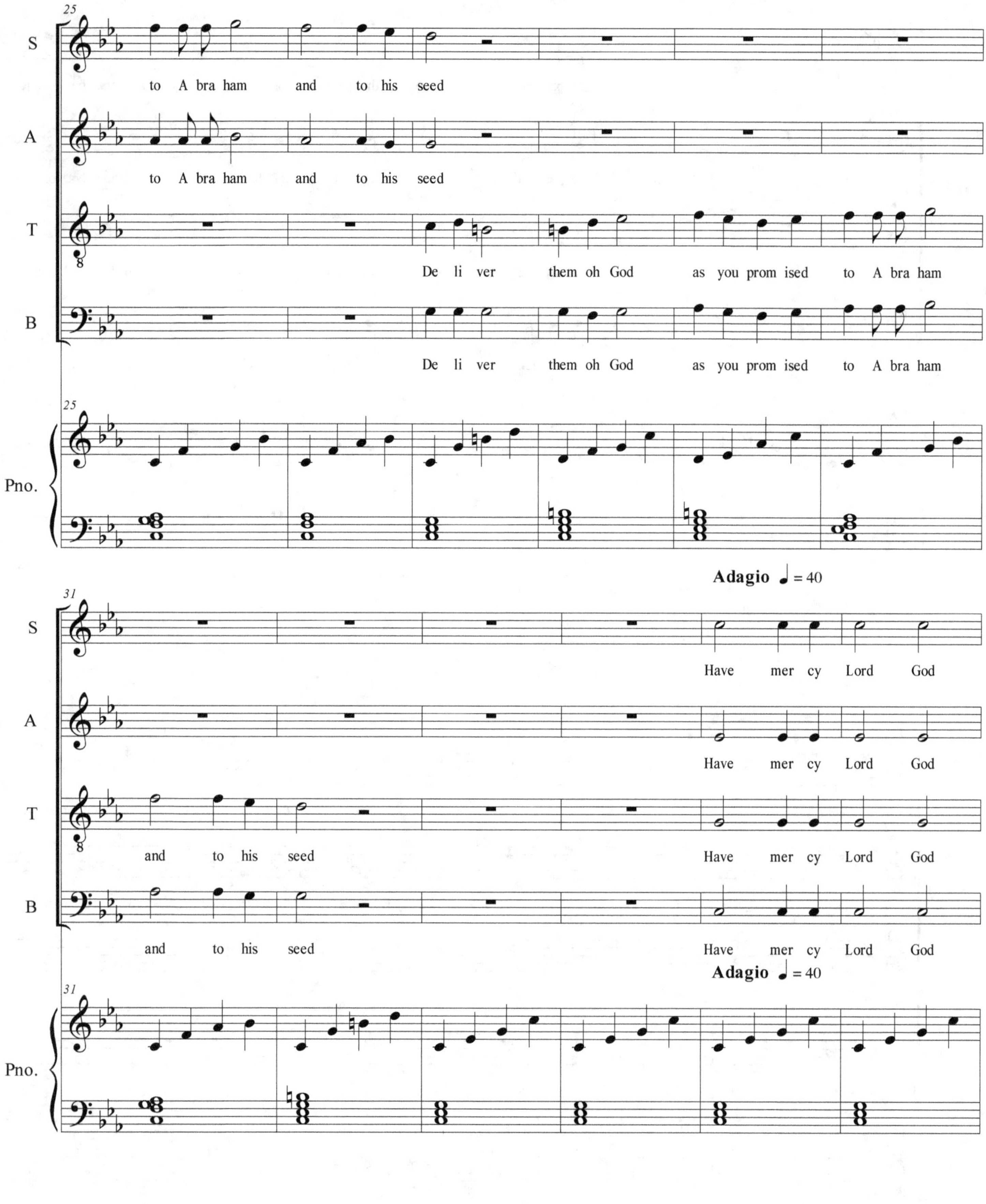
25
S
to A bra ham and to his seed
A
to A bra ham and to his seed
T
De li ver them oh God as you prom ised to A bra ham
B
De li ver them oh God as you prom ised to A bra ham
25
Pno.
Adagio ♩ = 40
31
S
Have mer cy Lord God
A
Have mer cy Lord God
T
and to his seed Have mer cy Lord God
B
and to his seed Have mer cy Lord God
Adagio ♩ = 40
31
Pno.

Offertorium

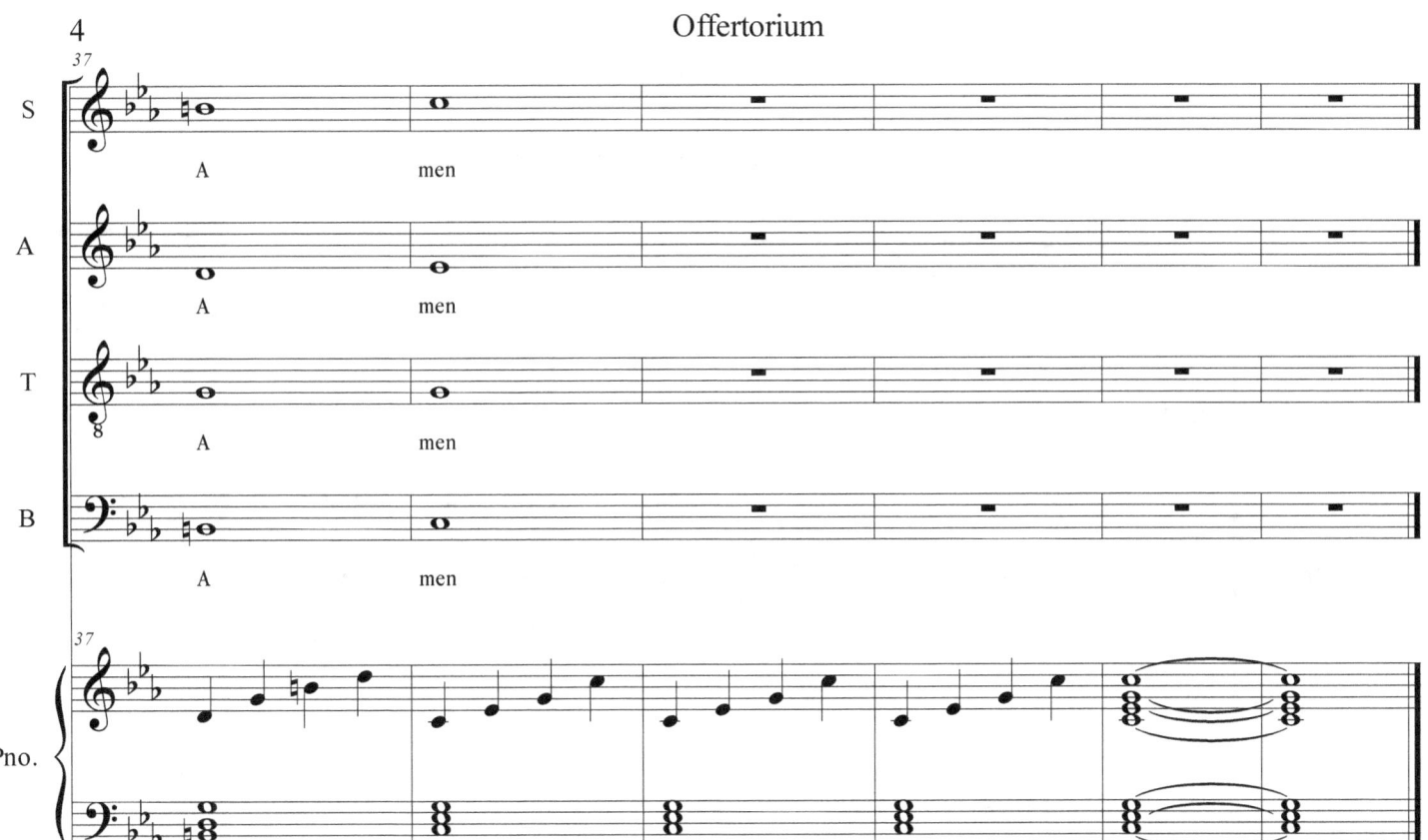

Sanctus
Requiem of Lost Souls

Kristina Howells

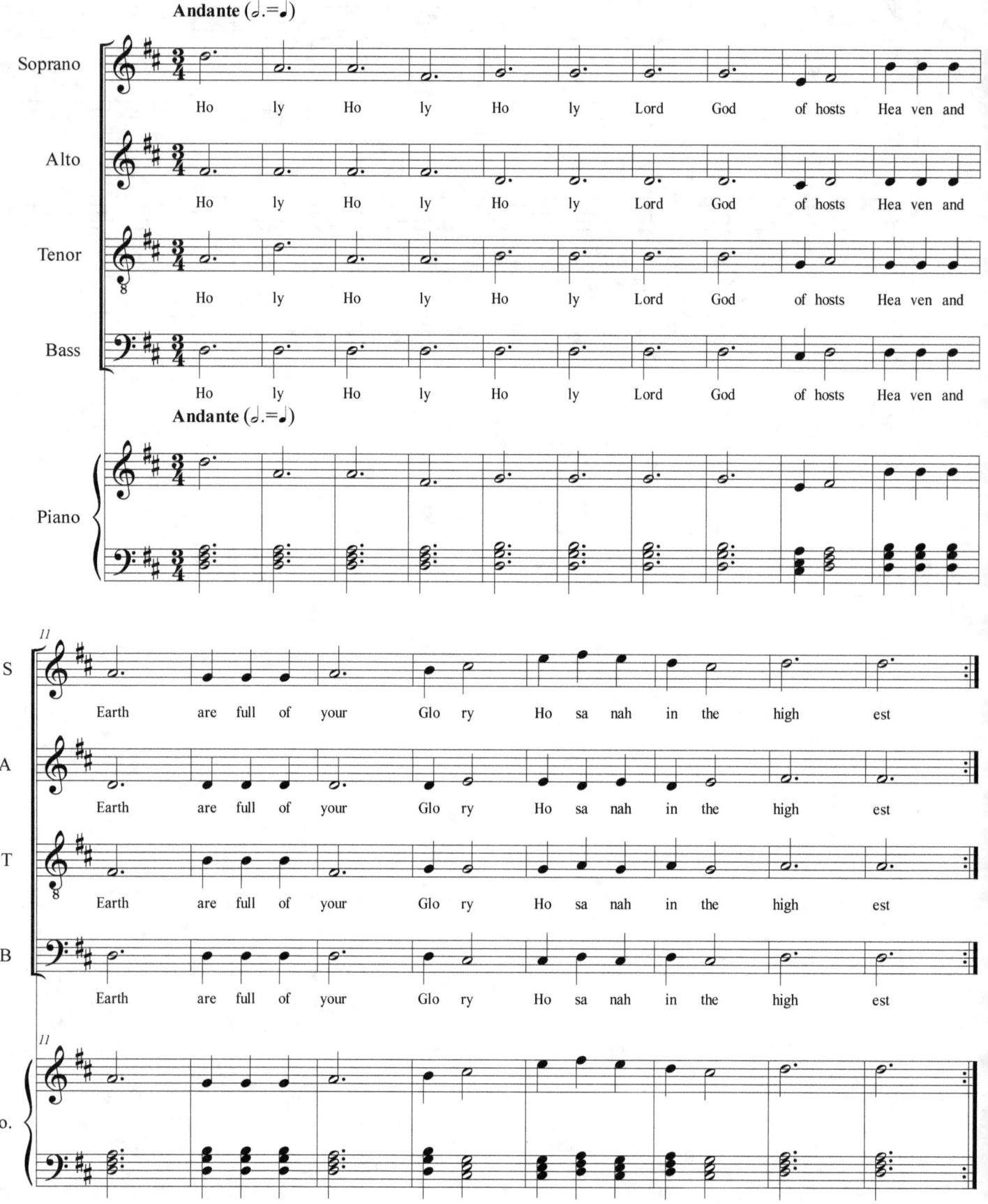

Oh Lamb of God

Requiem of Lost Souls

Kristina Howells

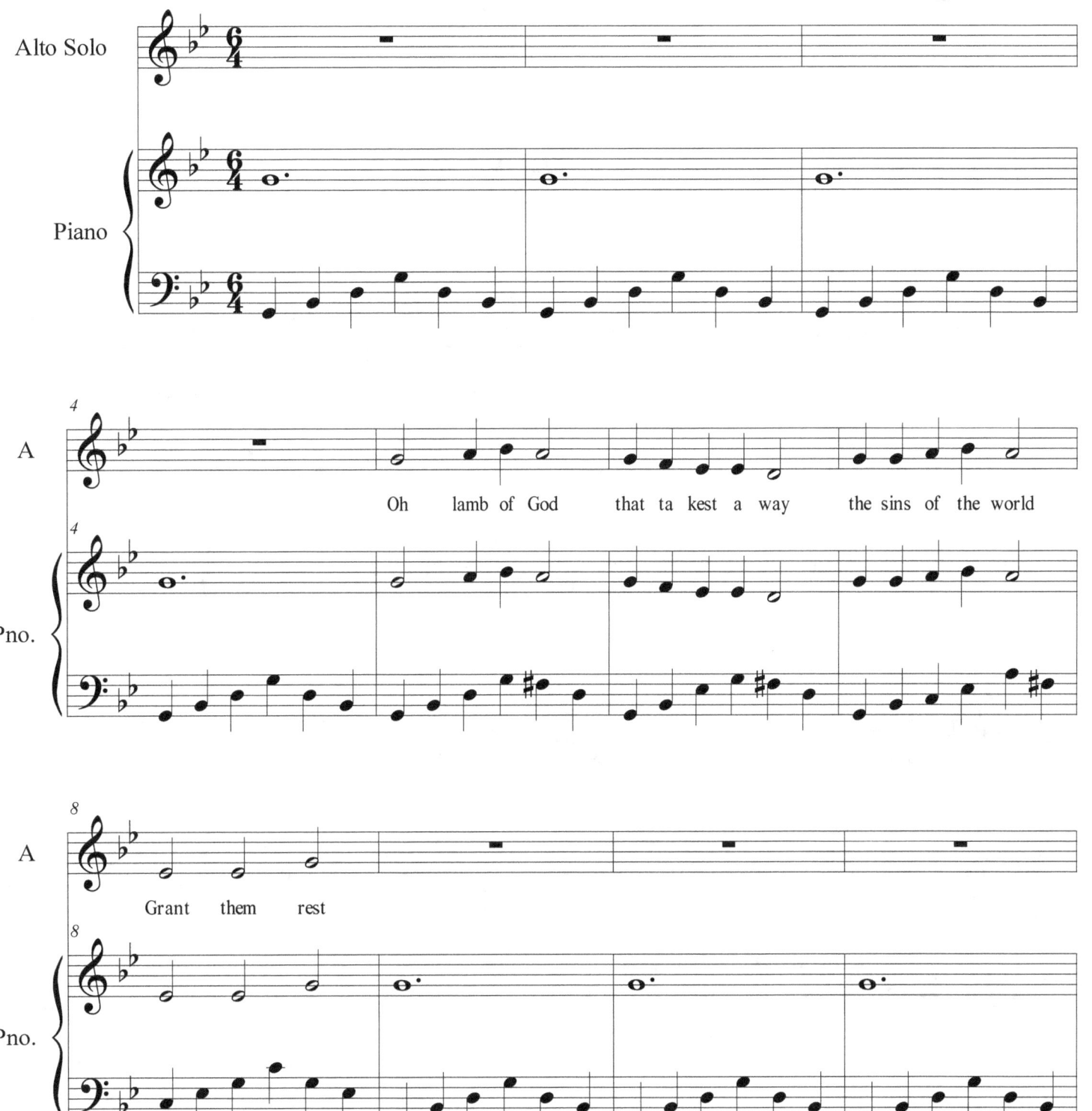

Oh lamb of God that ta kest a way the sins of the world

Grant them rest

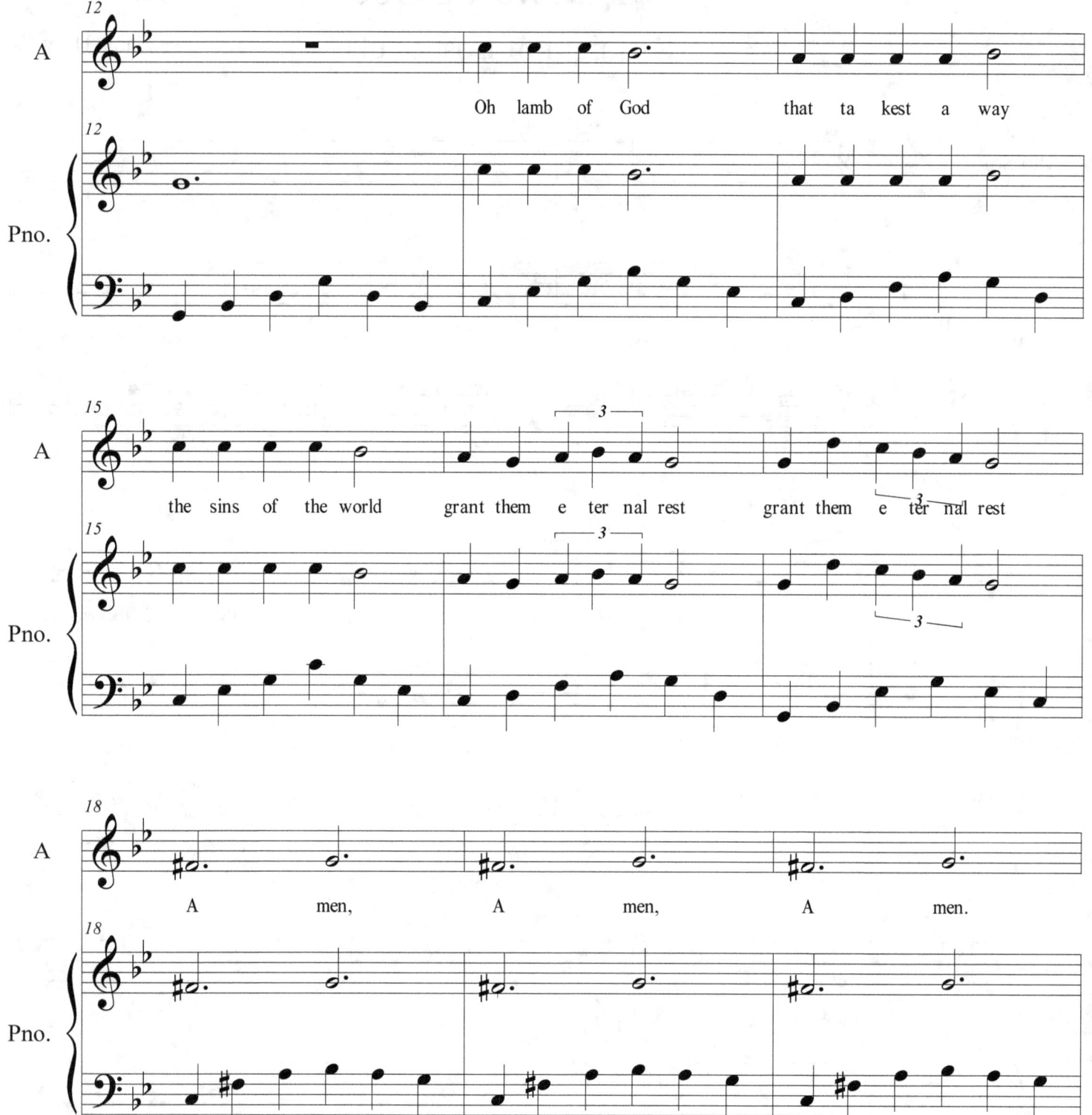

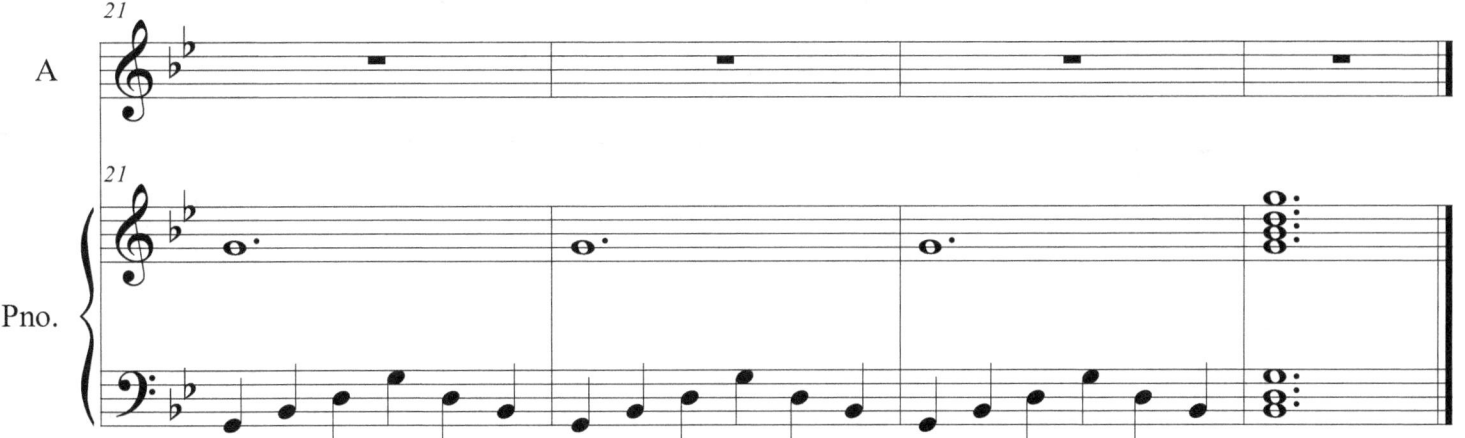

Liberame - Deliver us

Requiem of Lost Souls

Kristina Howells

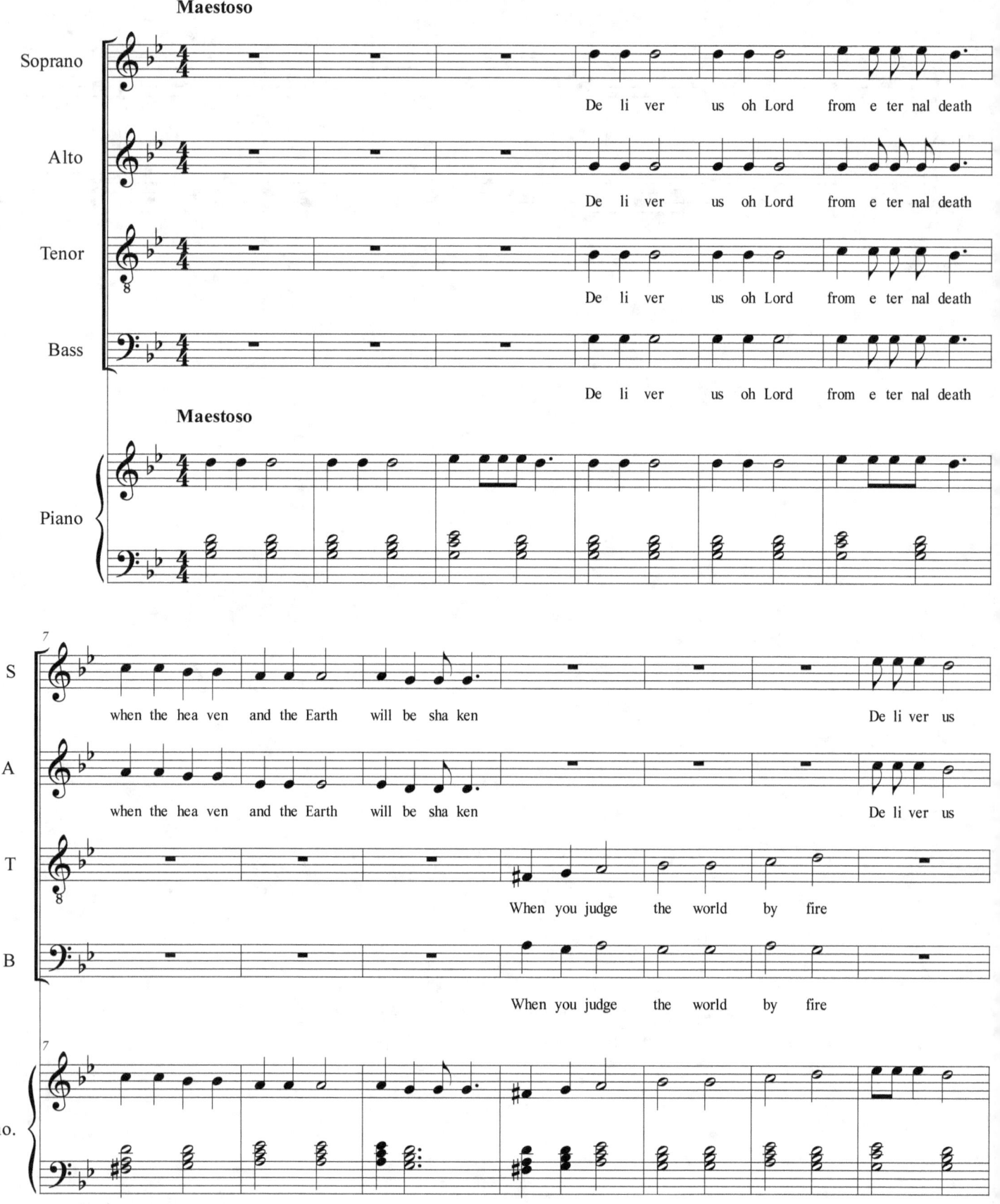

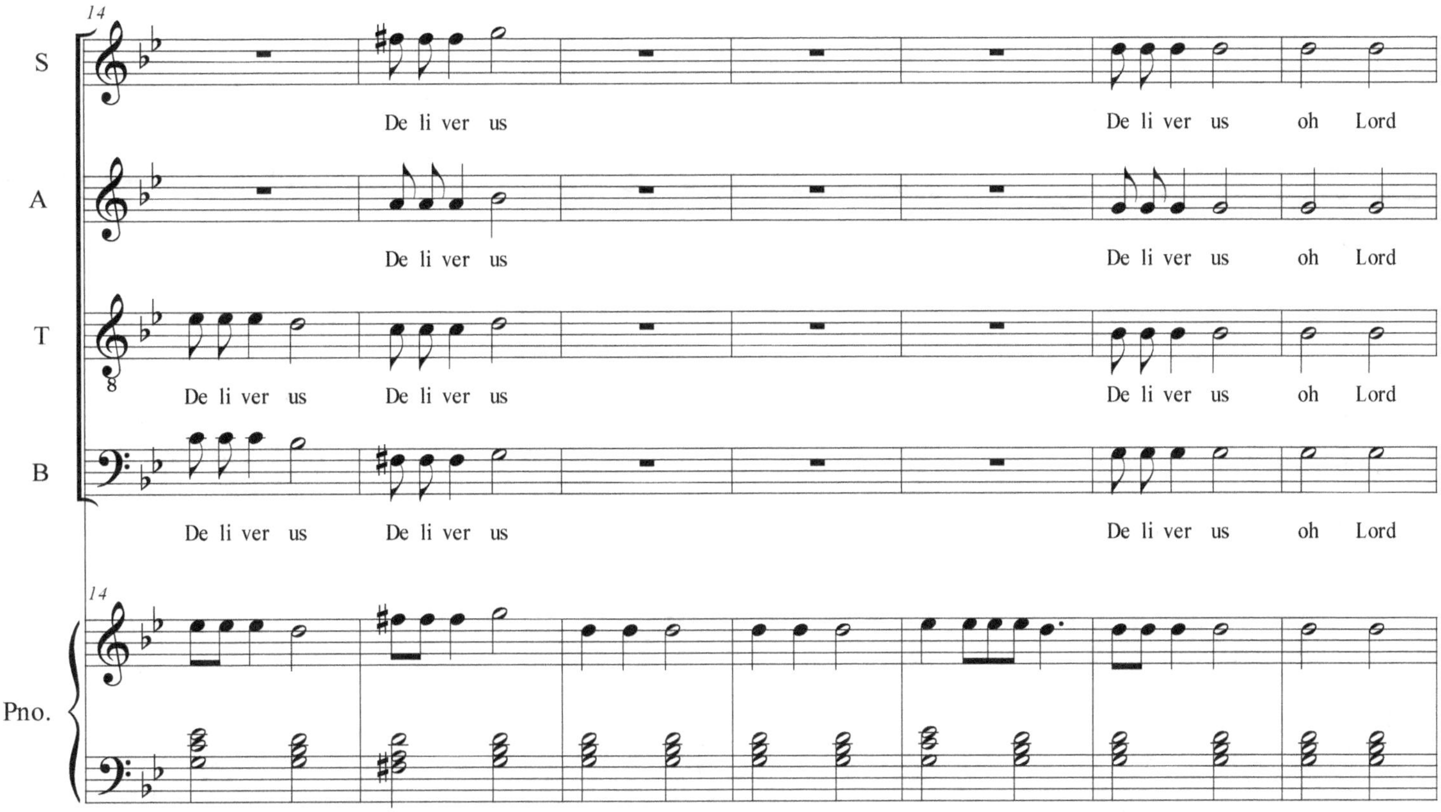

Liberame - Deliver us

S: De li ver us — De li ver us oh Lord

A: De li ver us — De li ver us oh Lord

T: De li ver us — De li ver us — De li ver us oh Lord

B: De li ver us — De li ver us — De li ver us oh Lord

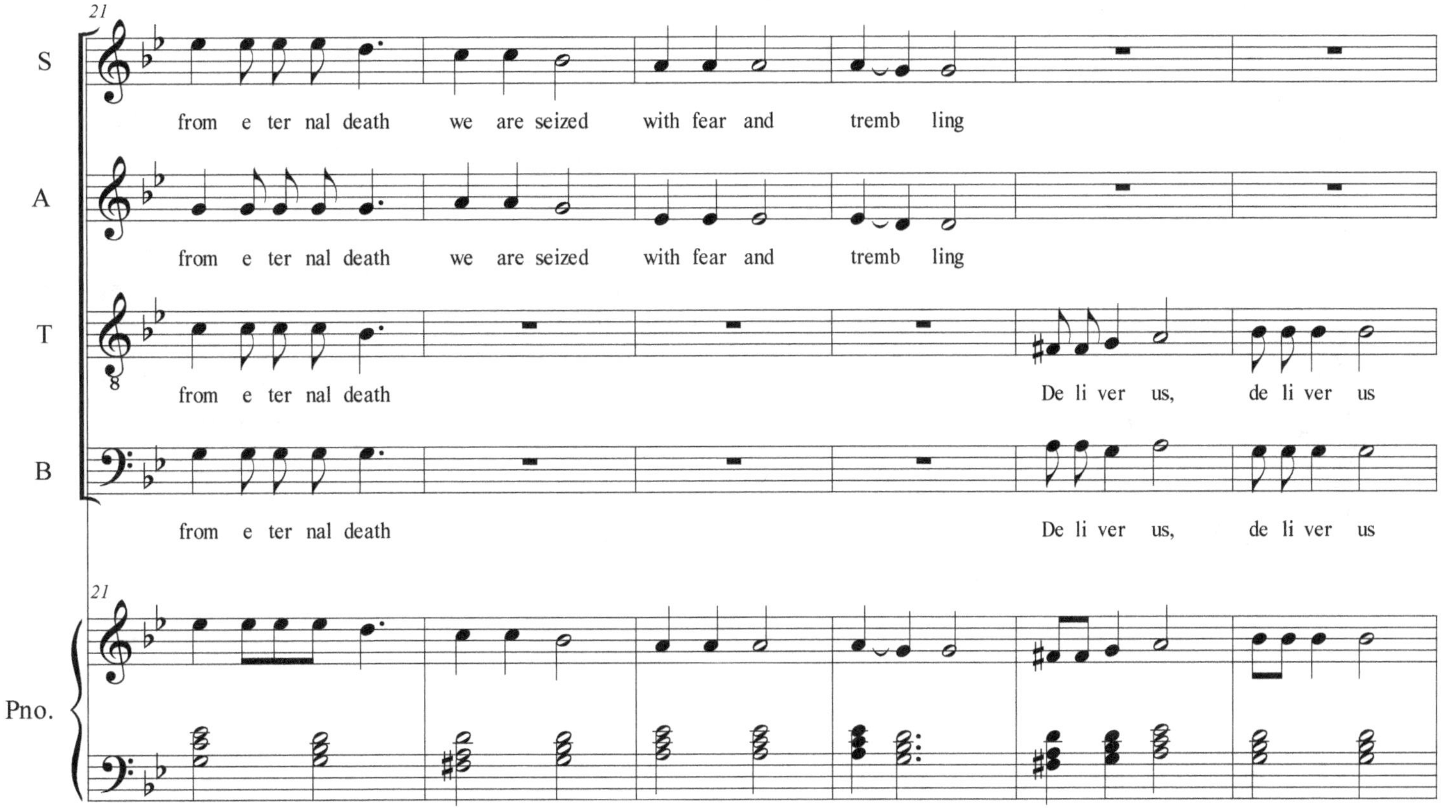

S: from e ter nal death — we are seized with fear and tremb ling

A: from e ter nal death — we are seized with fear and tremb ling

T: from e ter nal death — De li ver us, de li ver us

B: from e ter nal death — De li ver us, de li ver us

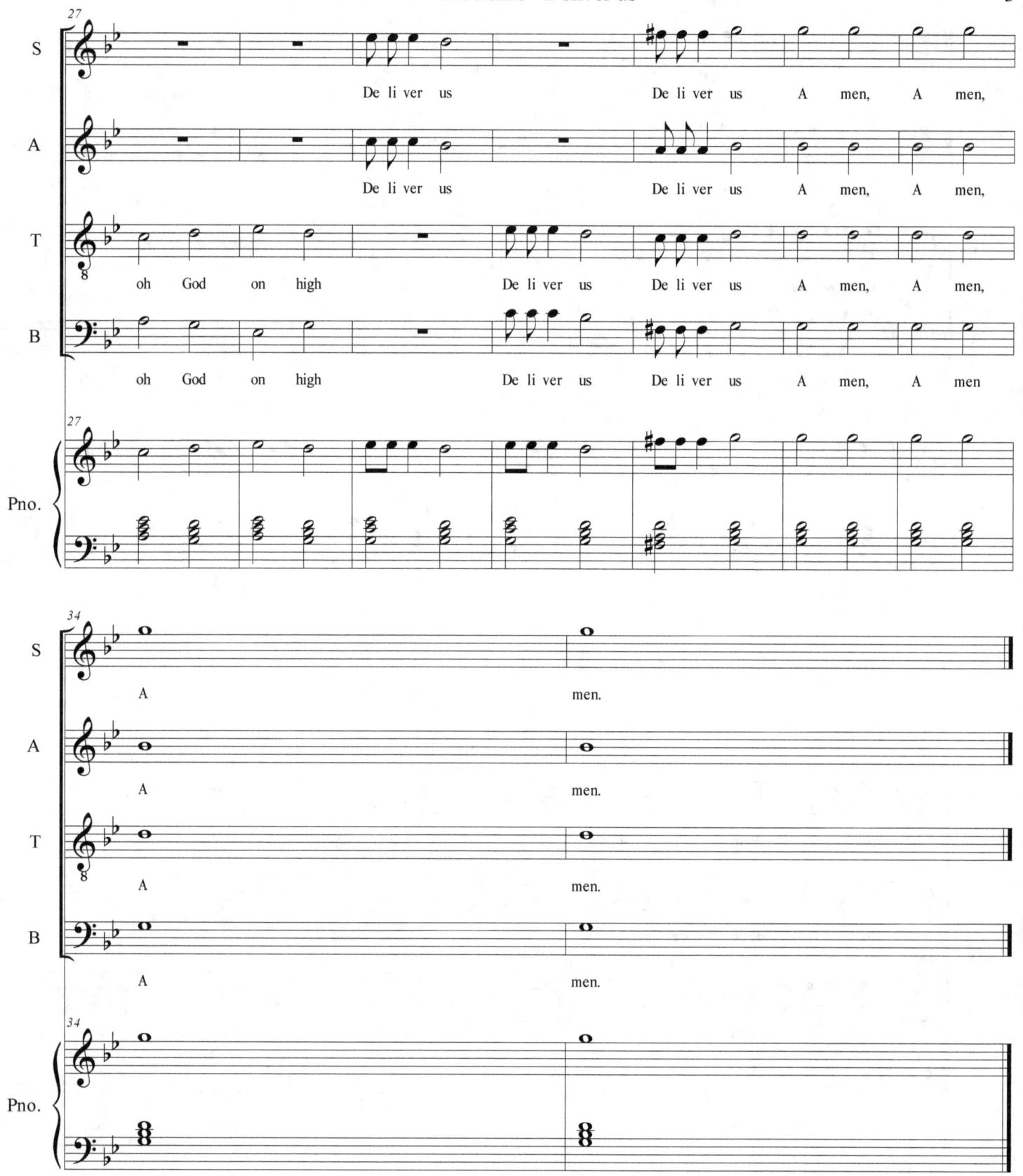